Edible Secrets

D1296712

Michael Hoerger & Mia Partlow

Edible Secrets: A Food Tour of Classified US History
by Michael Hoerger & Mia Partlow

Paperback: 128 pages
Publisher: Microcosm Publishing
Language: English
ISBN-10: 1934620416
ISBN-13: 978-1934620410

Microcosm Publishing
222 S Rogers St.
Bloomington, IN 47404-4936
812.232.7395
www.microcosmpublishing.com

Microcosm hQ Store
636 SE 11th Ave.
Portland, OR 97214

Illustrations by Nate Powell
(Front and back cover; chapter beginnings; pages 7 and 105)
seemybrotherdance.org

Portions of chapter 3 published previously as the zine:
The Curious Case of the Communist Jell-O Box (Microcosm Publishing)

ediblesecrets.com

EDIBLE SECRETS

A FOOD TOUR OF
CLASSIFIED US HISTORY

MICHAEL HOERGER & MIA PARTLOW

Microcosm Publishing

Dedicated to the spirit of Fred Hampton
and those who left it all on the line
for a radically better world.

CONTENTS

CHAPTER 5
~~SECRET~~ CIA POPCORN

CHAPTER 6
~~CONFIDENTIAL~~ COCA-COLA LIAISON

CHAPTER 7
~~CONFIDENTIAL~~ COCA-COLA FIREBOMB

CHAPTER 8
~~SECRET~~ RONALD REAGAN BROWNIES & HYDROPONICS

So what is this? It is a collection of U.S. government documents that have been declassified. At one time they were Top Secret. Confidential. Very hush hush. Now, these documents have been declassified, sanitized, redacted, and made public by the government. All of the documents shown here have one common theme: food!

Why *Edible Secrets*? There are millions of pages of declassified government documents. If you've ever wanted to peek behind the door of a top secret government meeting, or wondered how they broach delicate topics such as corporate boycotts, mind control, espionage, and assassination attempts, these documents provide you a voyeuristic insight into the U.S. government. By using food as a filter, we have chosen a collection of documents that touch upon important and iconic people and narratives of the last century. Perhaps all of these *Edible Secrets* are a testament to the obvious: food is everywhere. Or maybe they say the same thing about secrecy in our government?

Bon Appétit,
Michael & Mia

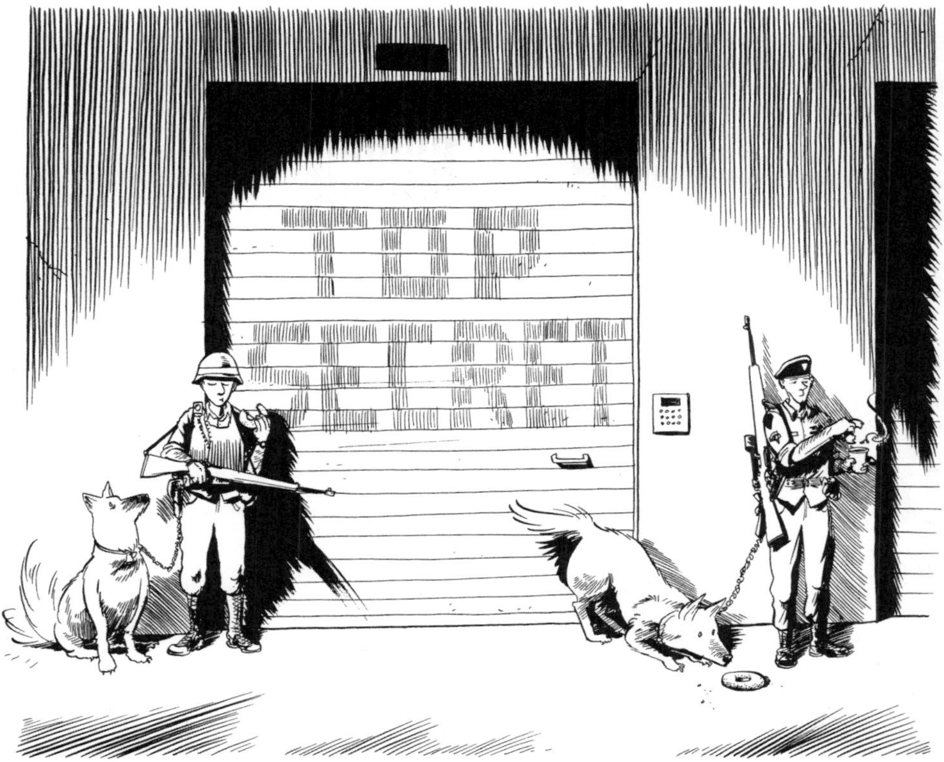
TOP
SECRET

1

~~SECRET~~ DOUGHNUTS

THE DOCUMENT

This memo is a redacted intelligence briefing written for President Dwight Eisenhower and his staff in August of 1956. The item that stands out for not remaining classified in this document is a boastful note about the success of the American exhibit at the London Food Fair. 1,000 doughnuts per hour! Why keep that a secret?

UNCLASSIFIED
SECRET

OPERATIONS COORDINATING BOARD
Washington 25, D. C.

2361

30 August 1956

INTELLIGENCE NOTES

1. Panama – Panama Canal

Panama's President and the President-elect recently agreed that the next administration will "harp constantly" on Panama's "irrevocable sovereignty" over the Panama Canal. CIA comments that such a campaign would be designed to weaken US treaty rights and gain ultimate participation in the operation and profits of the canal.

2. Great Britain – London Food Fair

The London Food Fair opened Tuesday to capacity crowds. US Embassy London reports the American exhibit, which is the largest in the fair, is a full-fledged hit with doughnuts being distributed at the rate of 1,000 per hour. (US Embassy London 1154, 29 August, Unclassified)

3. Egypt – Military Needs

4783581
4783591
1
1 – Wm. H. Jackson – EOB
4783601 – A P Toner – Wh. House

Aug 31 9 2. PM '56

SECRET

DECLASSIFIED WITH DELETIONS
E.O. 12356, SEC. 3.4(b)
Agency Case NLC F910403
NLE Case 90-272-8
By NLE

UNCLASSIFIED

5. Baghdad Pact - US Participation Recommended

US Embassy Ankara and USIS Baghdad have both recently commented that now is an appropriate time for the US to shore-up Western prestige in the Arab world by joining the Baghdad Pact. US Embassy Ankara believes that the effectiveness of the Baghdad Pact will be seriously endangered if Nasr emerges from the Suez crisis unscathed. (US Embassy Ankara 496, 28 August, Secret; USIS Baghdad TOUSI 70, 27 August, Confidential)

6. Cambodia - Possible Cambodian Recognition of North Vietnam

Prince Sihanouk confirmed ┊⁚⁚⁚⁚⁚⁚⁚⁚⁚⁚⁚⁚⁚⁚⁚⁚⁚⁚⁚⁚⁚⁚⁚┊ that any request made by North Vietnam for diplomatic representation in Cambodia will be accepted in spite of South Vietnamese objections. ┊⁚⁚⁚⁚⁚⁚⁚⁚┊ ┊⁚⁚⁚⁚South Vietnam will not withdraw its representative from Phnom Penh, but the issue is potentially explosive as it is felt in Saigon that Sihanouk's attitude is one of bad faith. ┊⁚⁚⁚⁚⁚⁚⁚⁚⁚⁚⁚⁚⁚⁚⁚┊

7. [text redacted]

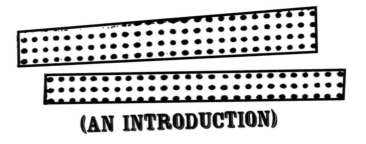

(AN INTRODUCTION)

When we began collecting documents for Edible Secrets, we had the feeling of being flies on the wall of secretive government offices, hearing things we weren't meant to, information that would take us days or weeks to decipher. But even among all of the documents that give us insights into nefarious government programs, the Secret Doughnuts Memo (page 10) quickly became a favorite of ours. We love how the note on the popularity of American doughnuts is tucked into a memo on international intelligence. We wonder if maybe there was a CIA intern who snuck the bullet in as a joke, or if there is a companion memo somewhere alerting bureaucrats that the President's spirits were down and some cheering up was in order. Ultimately, we just love how perfectly apt it is that the American exhibit was the largest at the international food fair and we love picturing doughnuts "being distributed at the rate of 1,000 per hour." If it weren't true, it would almost be trite.

But the Secret Doughnuts Memo is unlike the rest in this book. The London Food Fair and the popular American exhibit came and went without leaving much of a mark on the history of the 20th century. But as we began research on assassinations and acts of international espionage for the other chapters, we became more interested in what was missing from this document. The ambiguous but highly suggestive headings—Egypt's Military needs, etc—sent us into a frenzy of speculation. Ultimately, there is not enough information in the document itself to warrant its own chapter, but what the Secret Doughnuts Memo does show is that even 55 years later, many government efforts are still veiled in a shroud of secrecy.

The rest of the food items and declassified documents in this book help open up histories lost in the chaos of the last century. We have used food as a filter, a way to sort through the millions of declassified government documents. These public documents allow us to see history through a new lens, to disturb the popular narrative. And while many of the stories we tell in this book are well-known to scholars, often these histories do not trickle down, as it were, to the popular imagination.

Today, many of the U.S. government's classified documents undoubtedly deal with Al-Qaeda and the war on terror. The next three chapters of this book deal with the threat that overwhelmed a previous generation: communism.

In chapter two, we use a short weekly memo written by the Director of the FBI to reveal the history of the FBI and the Black Panther Party. In this declassified document, a short note about a nonviolent ice cream theft opens up an entire history of FBI surveillance that ends with the U.S. government's assassination of one of its own citizens.

In chapter three, we explore the Curious Case of the Communist Jell-O Box. This chapter illuminates the execution of Julius and Ethel Rosenberg for conspiracy to commit espionage as a ploy to instill fear and assert control over political thought and action in the United States. The threat of communism allowed McCarthy's show trials, forgeries, propaganda, and secret government agencies to go on for years—constraining the Left and other radical activists.

The document in chapter four, "Secret Chocolate Milkshake," is evidence of only one of over six hundred attempts by the United States government to assassinate Cuban leader Fidel Castro. In a secret meeting with Castro, a Pentagon official readily admits the U.S. government tried to poison Castro's chocolate milkshake. Since a secret meeting between Cuba and the United States to negotiate the release of political prisoners is not within the bounds of the U.S. policy of nonengagement with Cuba, the press was informed that a U.S.-based group of Cuban expatriots negotiated the release of the prisoners. So in addition to being evidence of extra-legal offense against communism, the document is also a good lesson on how U.S. public policy does not always align neatly with the actions of the U.S. government.

Chapter five explores how an experiment with subliminal messaging is tied to the War on Terror through a secret history of human experimentation and the development of torture techniques within the U.S. intelligence community. Currently used by American interrogators in multiple theaters of war, many torture techniques, such as sensory deprivation, were originally part of a program called MKUltra. MKUltra is the thread that ties the war on communism to the War on Terror; interrogation techniques developed to fight communists are now being used in black prisons around the world.

Chapters six and seven highlight the most iconic of sugary American products: Coca-Cola. While chapters two through four highlight defense against the perceived communist threat, chapter six shows us the offensive—the spread of capitalism as foreign policy. Chapter seven explores the resistance to Coca-Cola as a symbol of American economic and cultural imperialism. Close ties between the U.S. government and the Coca-Cola Corporation are illustrated.

The final chapter looks at the legacy of Ronald Reagan, and, alongside yet another dessert, introduces the only health food in the book: hydroponic lettuce. Transcripts of meetings with foreign heads of state provide an intimate look into the reception Reagan received with his neoliberal policies.

All of these histories are essential to understanding the full picture of United States history in the last century. And as we attempt to understand the events unfolding in our current century, we must remember how much is kept secret from us. As this book goes to print, a website leaked nearly 100,000 pages of classified material related to the U.S. war in Afghanistan and 390,000 classified pages on the war in Iraq.

The polka-dots in the Secret Doughnuts memo remind us that we do not always know the truth. The U.S. government operates in great secrecy. But let the remaining documents' histories remind us that we must continue always to push forward through the darkness and fight for the things we know are right.

2

~~CONFIDENTIAL~~ FRED HAMPTON ICE CREAM

THE DOCUMENT

In 1968, FBI Director J. Edgar Hoover sent this memo to the highest offices in the Executive branch. The memo concentrates on "selected racial developments and disturbances," culled from news and intelligence sources around the country. Fred Hampton's arrest for the robbery and assault of a white ice cream truck driver is the third event described in the memo, which has been reproduced in its entirety.

DECLASSIFIED
E.O. 12356, Sec. 3.4
NIJ 95-149
By ___Ch___, NARA, Date 8-24-95

1130 AM 7-11-68 NSM
HPRIORITY   RECEIVED   CONFIDENTIAL
TO: THE PRESIDENT 001
TO: SECRETARY OF STATE 001
TO: DIRECTOR, CIA 001
TO: DIRECTOR, DEFENSE INTELLIGENCE AGENCY 1968 JUL 11 15 50
TO: DEPARTMENT OF THE ARMY 001
TO: DEPARTMENT OF THE AIR FORCE 0001
TO: WHITE HOUSE SITUATION ROOM, ATT.: SECRET SERVICE (PID)
FROM: DIRECTOR, FBI

C O N F I D E N T I A L

SELECTED RACIAL DEVELOPMENTS AND DISTURBANCES

DEMONSTRATORS FIGHT POLICE, NEW YORK CITY: AT CITY HALL IN
NEW YORK CITY YESTERDAY ABOUT ONE-THOUSAND FIVE HUNDRED NEGRO
AND PUERTO RICAN YOUTHS STAGED A WILD DEMONSTRATION DEMANDING
MORE JOBS. GANGS OF YOUTHS PUNCHED AND ROBBED BYSTANDERS, OVERTURNED
AND LOOTED STREET VENDERS' STANDS, VANDALIZED AUTOMOBILES, AND
RAINED BRICKS, BOTTLES, AND PIECES OF JAGGED GLASS ON POLICE. WHEN
ABOUT ONE HUNDRED FIFTY POLICE OFFICERS ATTEMPTED TO BREAK UP THE
END PAGE ONE

PAGE TWO ~~CONFIDENTIAL~~

UNRULY CROWD, A MELEE TOOK PLACE. FIREMEN RESPONDING TO A
FALSE FIRE ALARM WERE ATTACKED BY THE DEMONSTRATORS. A NUMBER OF
DEMONSTRATORS WERE ARRESTED. FIVE POLICE OFFICERS WERE INJURED,
ONE SERIOUSLY.

POLICE ATTACKED, LOS ANGELES, CALIFORNIA: OFFICERS OF THE HARBOR
DIVISION OF THE LOS ANGELES, CALIFORNIA, POLICE DEPARTMENT WERE
ATTACKED BY AN UNRULY CROWD OF SEVERAL HUNDRED PEOPLE YESTERDAY
WHEN THEY APPREHENDED AN AUTOMOBILE THEFT SUSPECT IN THE PREDOMINANTLY
NEGRO HARBOR CITY AREA. THE OFFICERS WERE INJURED AND ONE OF THE
INJURIES WAS CONSIDERED SERIOUS. ADDITIONAL UNITS OF THE HARBOR
DIVISION DISPATCHED TO THE SCENE OF THE DISORDER REMOVED THE INJURED
OFFICERS, DISPERSED THE CROWD, AND ARRESTED FOUR NEGRO MALES ON
CHARGES OF ASSAULT WITH A DEADLY WEAPON.

WHITE TRUCK DRIVER ATTACKED BY NEGROES, MAYWOOD, ILLINOIS: A
GROUP OF NEGRO YOUTHS IN MAYWOOD, ILLINOIS, ATTACKED A CAUCASIAN
ICE CREAM ROUTE TRUCK DRIVER YESTERDAY NEAR A PLAYGROUND. THE
DRIVER WAS BEATEN AND ROBBED AND ABOUT FIFTY DOLLARS WORTH OF ICE
CREAM WAS DESTROYED. AFTER TREATMENT AT A LOCAL HOSPITAL, THE DRIVER
END PAGE TWO

PAGE THREE   C O N F I D E N T I A L
RETURNED TO THE PLAYGROUND WITH POLICE AND IDENTIFIED FRED ALLEN
HAMPTON AS THE INDIVIDUAL WHO LED THE ASSAULT. HAMPTON IS A
MILITANT BLACK NATIONALIST AND IS PRESIDENT OF THE WEST
SUBURBAN CHAPTER OF THE NATIONAL ASSOCIATION FOR THE
ADVANCEMENT OF COLORED PEOPLE YOUTH COUNCIL. HAMPTON WAS
CHARGED WITH ROBBERY, CRIMINAL DAMAGE TO PROPERTY, AND BATTERY.
HE WAS RELEASED ON FOUR THOUSAND DOLLARS BOND.

POOR PEOPLE'S CAMPAIGN: IN WASHINGTON, D. C., A POOR PEOPLE'S
CAMPAIGN RALLY WAS CANCELLED YESTERDAY BECAUSE OF LACK OF
ATTENDANCE. THE SECURITY DEPARTMENT OF THE CAMPAIGN, WHICH
REPORTEDLY HAS "FALLEN APART," IS BEING REORGANIZED. OTHER
CAMPAIGN ACTIVITIES ARE BEING GENERALLY SUSPENDED UNTIL RALPH D.
ABERNATHY, CAMPAIGN LEADER, IS RELEASED FROM JAIL ON JULY
THIRTEEN, NINETEEN SIXTY EIGHT. EFFORTS ARE BEING MADE TO
MOBILIZE A LARGE CONTINGENT TO BE PRESENT WHEN ABERNATHY IS
RELEASED.
GP-1
END

A SHRINER, 70, AND HIS BRIDE AT CONVENTION

Call It Ideal Place for a Honeymoon

BY PATRICIA KRIZMIS

Unlike most newlyweds who want to be alone, Gordon S. Wallschlaeger, 70, and his bride are spending their honeymoon with 125,000 Shriners.

Now a Shriners' convention may not be every girl's dream for a honeymoon, but Hattie Wallschlaeger, 76, said yesterday: "It is just great. Everyone in Chicago is wonderful."

She's a June Bride

Hattie became Mrs. Gordon Wallschlaeger June 22. And she and her husband, a member of Milwaukee's Tripoli temple, decided the 94th annual Shrine convention would be ideal for a honeymoon.

"But Sunshine [Wallschlaeger's nickname for his bride] and I have a good time any place we go," said Wallschlaeger, owner of a construction company and a building products firm in Milwaukee.

"I'm so proud of her," he said, looking at the petite gray-haired woman. "I've been introducing her to many of the Shriners and their wives."

Widow 19 Years

Ask her about her new family, and Hattie Wallschlaeger begins a lengthy discussion about her "Gordy" and his son and daughter.

"I never had any children of my own," said Mrs. Wallschlaeger, who was a widow for 19 years. "Now I have a whole new family plus six darling grandchildren."

Wallschlaeger's first wife died in May, 1967.

Wallschlaeger met Hattie in January.

"We had quite an unusual meeting," he said. "I was trying to contact friends of

[TRIBUNE Staff Photo]

Shrine Honeymooners

Gordon Wallschlaeger and his wife, Hattie, who are honeymooning at Shrine convention.

'Shrine Priest' Cites Works of Fraternity

The Shriners are a Masonic fraternity, but last night a priest told of thousands of Catholics who have offered prayers, lighted candles, and attended masses for the nobles in gratitude for their good works.

Rev. Joseph Steckler, pastor of St. Peter Catholic church in Linton, Ind., spoke before

mine in a Milwaukee suburb by the name of Weaver. Hattie's name was Weaver before she married men. I accidentally reached her on the telephone. We talked for quite a while and the next time I was in the suburb I stopped to see her."

Native of Chicago

Wallschlaeger was born in Chicago, but his family moved to Wisconsin when he was a child.

"Chicago's a fine place for a honeymoon," he said. "And Sunshine is a fine woman—and a good cook."

Shriners gathered for a dinner in the Conrad Hilton hotel.

Known as "the Shriner priest," Father Steckler is chairman of the nobles' ecumenical board. He has supported the fraternity for years because of their work with crippled children and burns victims, something of which he has first-hand knowledge.

Gets 9 Operations

Father Steckler was born with a club foot. He was an invalid until the Shriners learned of his case and brought him to their hospital in St. Louis, one of 19 institutions they operate for underprivileged crippled children thruout the nation.

After 11 years and nine major operations, Father Steckler regained the use of his leg and he went on to fulfill his lifelong dream of entering the priesthood.

"As long as I live," he said, "I shall be eternally grateful to the man who wears the scimitar on the lapel and the red fez which he wears proudly on his head.

Cites Work for All

"Not only for what the Shriners have done for me, but for what they have done for more than 150,000 children in the last 45 years who suffered the plight I did.

"Let us not forget that before we are Catholics, Protestants, Jews, Shriners, or Masons, we are human beings. We all dedicate ourselves to God. How you serve Him is your privilege."

Half Century Story: What's Best in Fez

By SHEILA WOLFE

Anyone who thinks a fez is just a fez ought to have a chat with Mrs. Rachelle Gadol. Fezzes have been her business for 50 years and she can spot a good one "a mile away."

Mrs. Gadol, who exercises a woman's prerogative and gives her age as 78, is among an estimated 55 exhibitors who are selling a wide range of products to Shriners and their families in the Shrine Market Place in the Palmer House.

Seated in a booth lined with fezzes, Mrs. Gadol watches all the fezzes go by with professional interest. Some like them plain, some like them fancy, she observed. There are those who prefer short tassels and those who favor long tassels. Mrs. Gadol has made all kinds.

"I always come up with something new," she said. "Back 50 years ago I used to hand make silk fezzes and each one took two days."

Mrs. Gadol was hard pressed to calculate how many fezzes she has made over the years. The best estimate is at least 20 a month.

All Shriners receive a free fez when they are inducted into

Mrs. Rachelle Gadol

something a bit more fancy.

Some fez facts: the price ranges from $9 to $75, depending on the quality; the weight is in the tassle; some hats are imported from Europe, as are some jewels; styles cannot change too drastically; a new type fez takes two to three months to plan and produce.

To Mrs. Gadol, whose son, Buddy, owns the family embroidery firm in New York, it is the workmanship that counts. She is proud of the fez she made for Buddy. But her real grooming glow is evident

The leader of a Maywood N. A. A. C. P. group was arrested last night on charges he led a band of youths in beating and robbing the driver of an ice cream truck.

Maywood police said the driver was assaulted at 16th and Warren avenues in the suburb by a group of 15 to 20 Negro youths. The driver, Nelson Suitt, 19, of 6200 Menard av., said the youths demanded ice cream, but refused to pay for it.

Driver Resists Pressure

He said when he told them he could not give them ice cream without receiving payment for it, they warned him, "Don't you know you are in a black power neighborhood?"

Suitt said he continued to resist the gang of toughs until one of them said, "Now you're going to have to give

us the ice cream—here comes our leader."

At this point, Suitt said, Fred Hampton, 19, of 804 S. 17th av., president of the youth council of the Maywood National Association for the Advancement of Colored People, drove up.

Climb Into Truck

Suitt said Hampton got into the cab of the Good Humor company ice cream truck and began to beat him. When Suitt was successful in shoving Hampton from the truck, the driver said, the rest of the gang joined in and beat him.

They broke all the windows of the truck and took his load of ice cream and his coin changer.

The driver flagged down a passing police car after the beating and robbery. Maywood police drove with Suitt near the scene of the crime and Suitt picked out Hampton as he walked on the street. Hampton was charged with

robbery, criminal damage to property, and battery. He was held in $4,000 bond for appearance Aug. 2 in West District court in Oak Park.

Hampton was involved in racial disorders in Maywood last September.

Fred Hampton's arrest was reported on page 4 of the Chicago Tribune (11 July 1968.)
The story was buried on a page devoted to local Shriner news.

BY ANY MEANS NECESSARY

FRED HAMPTON AND THE FBI'S
ILLEGAL WAR ON THE BLACK PANTHER PARTY

When Fred Hampton was arrested at age nineteen for stealing $71 worth of ice cream, he knew that the local police were falsely accusing him of the crime to get him into the criminal justice system. As the president of the Maywood, Illinois NAACP Youth Council, Hampton understood that his charisma—his ability to inspire, to articulate the myriad ways oppression affected the people—made him a target of the local police.

What Hampton did not know, and had no way of knowing, was that he had been an FBI target since he was fourteen years old. Nor was he aware that his arrest for the theft of ice cream had been reported by FBI Director J. Edgar Hoover to the President of the United States, the Secretary of State, the Director of the CIA, and even the Air Force.

Fred Hampton was, from a very young age, actively targeted by the FBI's Counter Intelligence Program, or COINTELPRO, an FBI program designed "to expose, disrupt, discredit, or otherwise neutralize the activities" of Black leaders.

On the local level, Chicago newspapers treated the ice cream arrest as a curiosity—if they covered it at all. The Chicago Tribune gave it 300 words on page four; The Defender—Chicago's African-American paper—did not even report the arrest. But it was reported to the highest officials in the United States government.

Fred Hampton speaking; October 1969.

Two years after his arrest, Hampton was convicted of the robbery and sentenced to two to five years in prison for the crime. Throughout the trial and sentencing Hampton maintained his innocence, testifying he had been mowing the lawn at the time. Indeed, there is a man still living in Hampton's Chicago neighborhood who claims to have robbed the ice cream truck; according to Hampton's lawyer, Jeffrey Haas, the man bears a striking resemblance to Hampton. Other than the testimony of the driver, who was flown in from his tour of duty in Vietnam to testify at the 1969 trial, there is no evidence supporting the state's allegation that Hampton committed the crime. When we contacted the ice cream truck driver, he had no comment.

There are, however, reams of government documents detailing the extent of the FBI's quest to bring all Black Power activists into the system, including hundreds of documents detailing the extent of their surveillance of Fred Hampton from the age of fourteen.

The FBI targeted leaders, and there was no question Fred had a natural leadership ability. At the time of his arrest he was head of the NAACP Youth Council, and months later, Fred began to emerge as a great leader—capable of bringing ordinary people out at six a.m. to do calisthenics and serve breakfast to local children.

Being framed in the ice cream truck robbery led to Fred's views

FRED HAMPTON SPEAKS

```
If you think about me and you think about me niggers and
you ain't gonna do no revolutionary act then forget about
me.  I don't want myself on your mind if you're not going
to work for the people.
...
You have to understand that people have to pay the price
for peace.  You dare to struggle, you dare to win.  If you
dare not struggle, then gad dammit you don't deserve to
win.  Let me say to you peace if you're willing to fight
for it.
...
I believe I'm going to do my job ...  I don't believe I'm
going to die in a car wreck.  I don't believe I'm going to
die slipping on a piece of ice.  I don't believe I'm going
to die because I have a bad heart.  I don't believe I'm
going to die because I have lung cancer.

I believe I'm going to be able to die doing the things I
was born for.  I believe I'm going to die high off the
people.  I believe I'm going to die a revolutionary in the
international revolutionary proletarian struggle.  I hope
each one of you will be able to die in the international
revolutionary proletarian struggle, or you'll be able to
live in it.  And I think that struggle's going to come.

Why don't you live for the people.
Why don't you struggle for the people.
Why don't you die for the people.
```

becoming increasingly radicalized. Among other things, his false arrest motivated him to start a Chicago chapter of the Black Panther Party and engage in revolutionary politics dedicated not only to Black Power, but power for all marginalized peoples.

As the head of Chicago's Black Panther Party, he formed the Rainbow Coalition to ally Chicago's gangs in solidarity against poverty. He negotiated gang truces, easing tension between races, and recruited gang members to help run the Panther Party's social programs and free breakfasts. Hampton even enlisted young white Appalachian men—also marginalized—as bodyguards.

Just before his murder at age twenty-one, Fred Hampton was in line to become the national Chairman of the Central Committee of the Black Panther Party. He was recognized for politicizing apolitical people, for giving them the tools to analyze their own oppression. It is no wonder he was considered such a threat to the United States government.

The Fred Hampton Ice Cream document has never before been published, primarily because Hampton biographies revolve around his assassination and the extreme breach of justice it represents.

If we take a different view, and reorient our perspective so that his murder was the culmination of a political life, we can see that there also existed a shadow version of his life, created by FBI documents, reports by informants, and false arrests. This surveillance led to his assassination, which was not an isolated incident in his life, but the culmination of a series of repressions and the outcome of an explicit government policy to suppress the Black Power movement.

Fred Hampton was assassinated on December 4, 1969 after an early morning raid on his Chicago apartment conducted jointly by the FBI and the Chicago Police Department. The police, armed with machine guns, shot over 90 bullets into the apartment before entering.

Fred's bodyguard, William O'Neal, was an FBI informant and agent-provocateur. He provided the FBI a detailed floor plan of Hampton's apartment, with Hampton's bed clearly marked.

O'Neal drugged Hampton on the evening prior so Hampton would not wake up during the raid. Even so, Hampton survived the machine gun fire. Fellow Black Panther Mark Clark was killed during the raid.

As gunfire abated and police entered the apartment, everyone still alive—besides Fred—was pushed into the kitchen including Fred's partner, Deborah Johnson—who was eight and a half months pregnant with Fred Hampton, Jr—heard two gun shots from Hampton's bedroom.

Sure to haunt her for years to come, she heard an officer state "he's good and dead now."

The U.S. government claims to have raided the apartment looking for an illegal weapons cache. There were no illegal weapons, and the use of informant William O'Neal to drug Fred and provide a map to his bed shows the raid was conducted specifically to assassinate Hampton.

The less traumatic episodes of Fred Hampton's life go unexamined because the lessons activists can learn from his false arrest for an ice cream robbery seem inconsequential compared to what was learned from his

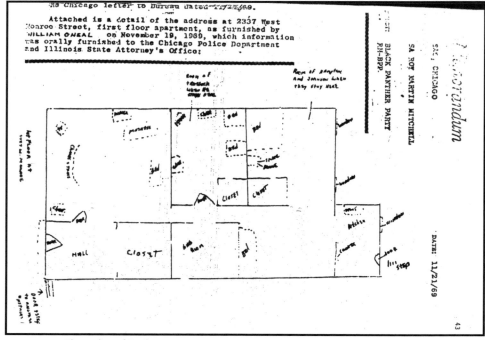

Floor plan of Fred Hampton's apartment supplied to the FBI by informant William O'Neal.

murder. But the document here shows that the ice cream robbery was a tactic, or at the very least—an opportunity for the U.S. government. And these tactics—the shadow life created by government surveillance—are still common today.

Developed as part of COINTELPRO, false arrests and the use of informants are widely still used against activists. These tactics have a history visible in this memo. While similar, the methods are not the same. The graphic on page 26 shows that for the Panthers, heavy-handed government repression included assault, harassment, imprisonment, and murder of members of an organization the FBI estimated at no more than 800 members in 1969.

Race enabled the government to be extremely blatant in its repression of the Black Power movement. But regardless of how blatant the repression, the U.S. government's use of informants, grand juries convened in a shroud of secrecy, threats of imprisonment to induce people to talk, and other tactics continues.

THE WAR ON THE PANTHERS

During the late 1960s and early 1970s, the FBI waged what can be fairly described as a domestic war on the Black Panther Party. Collaborating with state and local forces, the FBI used a variety of tactics to completely dismantle the Panthers. From misinformation to false arrests, from violent harassment to murder, no tactic was too subtle or too outrageous for the United States government's War on the Panthers.

Heavy political repression distracted Black Panther Party members from their community work. Funds raised for children's free breakfast programs were diverted to jail bonds and bail. Energy better spent organizing in their communities was instead spent on self-defense training. The FBI planted informants, provocateurs, and misinformation, which ended in chaos, infighting, and even murder. Ultimately, the Panthers could not match the unlimited resources and man-power of the U.S. government.

In February 1970 the Black Panther Party's official newspaper published a special report, "Evidence of Intimidation and Fascist Crimes by U.S.A." The paper had meticulously collected information from Party chapters across the country to create an account of every act of political repression against the Panthers. Depicted here are acts of repression from 1968 until the murders of Mark Clark and Fred Hampton in December, 1969.

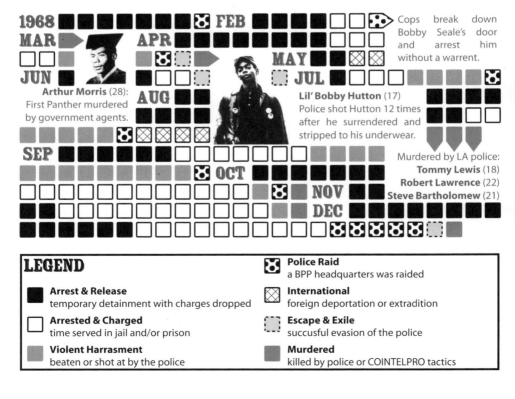

1968 ... **FEB** ... Cops break down Bobby Seale's door and arrest him without a warrent.

MAR ... **APR** ... **MAY** ...

JUN ... **JUL** ...

Arthur Morris (28): First Panther murdered by government agents.

AUG ...

Lil' Bobby Hutton (17) Police shot Hutton 12 times after he surrendered and stripped to his underwear.

SEP ...

OCT ...

NOV ...

DEC ...

Murdered by LA police:
Tommy Lewis (18)
Robert Lawrence (22)
Steve Bartholomew (21)

LEGEND

🔲 **Police Raid**
a BPP headquarters was raided

■ **Arrest & Release**
temporary detainment with charges dropped

☒ **International**
foreign deportation or extradition

☐ **Arrested & Charged**
time served in jail and/or prison

⬚ **Escape & Exile**
succusful evasion of the police

■ **Violent Harrasment**
beaten or shot at by the police

■ **Murdered**
killed by police or COINTELPRO tactics

1969

FEB

MAR

APR

New York 21:
21 Panthers in NYC were charged with conspiracy to bomb. Total bail was set at over $2,000,000. All were eventually acquitted.

MAY

Fred Hampton:
Sentenced to serve 2-5 years in prison for allegedly stealing $71 worth of ice cream.

JUN

Aircraft Piracy:
On separate occasions, William Lee Brent and Raymond Johnson successfully escape prison time and evade the police by hijacking planes to Cuba.

JUL

Welcome to **CUBA!**

AUG

SEP

Bobby Seale:
In order to demonize the Black Panther Party co-founder, a judge ordered Seale shackled and gagged in court, where he was facing charges of conspiracy and inciting a riot. The charges were eventually dropped.

OCT

Larry Roberson (20):
Coordinator of the Chicago BPP's Breakfast for Children program.

NOV

DEC

FREE THEM ALL!

BLACK PANTHERS BEHIND BARS

Over 100 political prisoners and prisoners of war are currently being held in United States prisons. One out of every five of these prisoners was at one time a member of the Black Panther Party.

Political prisoners are people who are more harshly charged, tried, and sentenced for crimes because of their political convictions, or people who have been falsely identified in order to stifle their political activities. Some Black Panther political prisoners are identified as "prisoners of war" because they were captured during their revolutionary struggle for Black Power.

Several of the Panthers' most inspiring leaders, including co-founder and Chairman Huey P. Newton and the young Fred Hampton, were in prison at the height of Panther activity in the late 1960s.

The Panthers supported their political prisoners and prisoners of war just as prior radical movements had, with letters, financial and legal support, and public statements made on behalf of the prisoner. In the 1950s, for example, the Left both in the U.S. and internationally provided this type of support for Julius and Ethel Rosenberg.

And today, the United States government continues to capture and hold political prisoners and prisoners of war, including Daniel McGowan, the Cuban 5, Marie Mason, and the San Francisco 8 (members of the Black Panther Party recently captured on forty-year old evidence and witness confessions given under duress), to name but a few. The names listed below are political prisoners and prisoners of war who were Black Panther Party members.

Many of these men have spent 30 to 40 years in prison for acting on their political beliefs. You are invited to write them and learn more about them and the movement to support political prisoners and the fight to free them all.

MUMIA ABU-JAMAL
#AM-8335
175 Progress Drive
Waynesburg, PA 15370-8090

SUNDIATA ACOLI (C. SQUIRE)
#39794-066
USP Otisville
P.O. Box 1000
Otisville, NY 10963

JAMIL ABDULLAH AL-AMIN
#99974-555
USP Florence ADMAX
P.O. Box 8500
Florence, CO 81226

ZOLO AGONA AZANIA
#4969
P.O. Box 41
Michigan City, IN 46361

HERMAN BELL
79C0262
Sullivan Correctional Facility
P.O. Box 116
325 Riverside Drive
Fallsburg, New York 12733-0116

VERONZA BOWERS JR.
#35316-136
P.O. Box 150160
Atlanta, GA 30315

MARSHALL EDDIE CONWAY
#116469
P.O. Box 534
Jessup, MD 20794

ROMAINE CHIP FITZGERALD
#B27527
Centinela State Prison
FC-2-110
PO Box 921
Imperial, California 92251-0731

ROBERT SETH HAYES
#74-A-2280
Wende Correctional Facility
3040 Wende Road
Alden, New York 14004-1187

FREDDIE HILTON (Kamau Sadiki)
#0001150688
Augusta State Medical Prison,
Bldg 13A-2 E7
3001 Gordon Highway
Grovetown, GA 30813

SEKOU KAMBUI (W. TURK)
#113058
P.O. Box 56 SCC (B1-21)
Elmore, AL 36025-0056

The United States of America would have you believe
that I am a criminal, that we all are criminals. That just
isn't so. I am a New Afrikan soldier, and we have an
absolute right to fight for our freedom. That is a
human right. That is not a right you have to ask or
beg for. Like all people who want to be free, what is
necessary to exercise that right is to stand up like
men and women and exercise it. If it calls for fighting,
then we fight.

- Sekou Odinga

For more information,
seek these groups out:
• The Jericho Movement
• Anarchist Black Cross
• ProLibertad
• 4 Struggle Magazine

MONDO WE LANGA (D. RICE)
#27768
P.O. Box 2500
Lincoln, NE 68542-2500

MALIKI LATINE
#81-A-4469
Clinton Correctional Facility
P.O. Box 2001
Dannemora, New York 12929

ABDUL MAJID
#83-A-0483
Elmira Correctional Facility
PO Box 500, 1879 Davis St
Elmira, New York 14902-0500

JALIL MUNTAQIM
(Anthony Bottom)
77A4283
Auburn CF
PO Box 618
Auburn, NY 13021

SEKOU ODINGA
09A3775
Downstate Correctional Facility
P.O. Box F
Fishkill, NY 12524

ED POINDEXTER
#27767
P. O. Box 2500
Lincoln, NE 68542

RUSSELL MAROON SHOATS
#AF-3855
175 Proggress Dr.
Waynesburg, PA 15370

RECOMMENDED READING:

The Assassination of Fred Hampton: How the FBI and Chicago Police Murdered a Black Panther
by Jeffrey Haas (Chicago, IL: Lawrence Hill Books, 2010)

The Murder of Fred Hampton
by Howard Alk and Mike Gray (DVD: Chicago, IL: Facets Multimedia, 1971)

Agents of Repression: The FBI's Secret Wars Against the Black Panther Party and the American Indian Movement
by Ward Churchill and Jim Vander Wall (Cambridge, MA: South End Press, 2002)

The Black Panthers Speak
edited by Philip S. Foner (Cambridge, MA: Da Capo Press, 1995)

Revolutionary Suicide
by Huey P. Newton (New York, NY: Harcourt Brace Jovanovich, 1973)

Let Freedom Ring: A Collection of Documents from the Movements to Free U.S. Political Prisoners
edited by Matt Meyer (Oakland, CA: PM Press, 2008)

The Black Panther Party: Service to the People Programs
by The Dr. Huey P. Newton Foundation (Albuquerque, NM: University of New Mexico Press, 2008)

The Black Panther Party [Reconsidered]
by Charles E. Jones (Baltimore, MD: Black Classic Press, 1998)

Black Power: Radical Politics and African American Identity
by Jeffrey Ogbonna Green Ogbar (Baltimore, MD: Johns Hopkins University Press, 2004)

From the Bottom of the Heap: The Autobiography of Black Panther Robert Hillary King
by Robert Hillary King (Oakland, CA: PM Press, 2009)

3

SECURITY INFORMATION:
COMMUNIST
JELL-O

THE DOCUMENT

After Julius and Ethel Rosenberg were convicted of conspiracy to commit espionage and sentenced to death in 1951, a pro-Rosenberg movement organized to appeal for clemency (a stay of execution) for the couple. In response, the CIA issued this internal memo, which reviews the government's case so rank-and-file Agents could counter local "pro-Rosenberg propaganda" and "Communist-inspired agitation" across the globe.

30 January 1953

MEMORANDUM FOR: CHIEFS, ALL AREAS AND DIVISIONS

SUBJECT: Refutation of Communist Charges in connection with the Rosenberg case.

1. Attached hereto is support material suitable for use by field stations in areas where it is necessary to counter pro-Rosenberg propaganda. It constitutes a concise and factual review of the Rosenberg case from its beginning up to the time of appeal for executive clemency.

2. The material is divided into seven sections.

    a. Government's case.

    b. Defendants' case.

    c. Government's Rebuttal.

    d. Conduct of the Trial.

    e. Verdict.

    f. Sentences.

    g. The Rosenberg Case and the Communist Party.

3. Inasmuch as Communist-inspired agitation in regard to the Rosenbergs will doubtless continue over a long period of time regardless of the outcome of their appeal for clemency, it is believed that this material will prove of continuing value to the field stations.

Attachment - 1
  As described

Distribution:

Security Information

LEGAL HISTORY

Julius and Ethel Rosenberg were indicted January 31, 1951, charged with conspiring between 1944 and 1950 to commit espionage. With them the Grand Jury indicted David Greenglass, Anatoli Yakovlev a Vice-Consul in the Soviet Consulate at New York, and Morton Sobell.

Greenglass pleaded guilty before the trial started. Yakovlev fled the country in 1946 but is still under indictment. Should he return to America, he would have to stand trial.

The trial of the two Rosenbergs and Sobell began on March 6, 1951. They were convicted on March 29, 1951. They were sentenced on April 5, 1951, the Rosenbergs to death by execution, Sobell to 30 years in jail.

From April 5 to date, the verdict and the sentence have been appealed several times to the Circuit Court of Appeals and to the Supreme Court. On February 25, 1952, the US Court of Appeals confirmed the lower court's decision and sentence. The Supreme Court of the United States refused to review the Court of Appeals' decision. The Rosenbergs and Sobell then moved in the District Court to set aside the jury's verdict. This motion was denied. The Rosenbergs and Sobell have appealed this denial, and this appeal is to be argued again in the Circuit Court of Appeals in a special session Dec. 22. This decision can also be appealed to the Supreme Court of the United States. The Rosenbergs and Sobell after that will be able to ask the District Court for a reduction of sentence. No appeal is possible from the decision on that request, and their final recourse will be an application to the President for executive clemency.

After the Rosenbergs and Sobell were convicted and sentenced, Greenglass was sentenced to serve 15 years in jail. Two persons were named in the original indictment as co-conspirators, but not defendants. They were Harry Gold, who pleaded guilty to a separate charge of espionage in Philadelphia and was sentenced to 30 years in prison, and Ruth Greenglass, the wife of David.

2.

A few days later Greenglass testified he went to Rosenberg's home for dinner and was introduced by Rosenberg to a woman named Ann Sidorovich. Greenglass testified Rosenberg asked him to remember her face because "Julius said this is the woman who he thinks would come out to see us at Albuquerque (where Mrs. Greenglass lived, near Los Alamos) to receive information from myself on the atomic bomb." Greenglass testified Rosenberg that night also established an alternate means of identification between Greenglass and Rosenberg's representative in case Ann Sidorovich was unable to travel. This alternate means of identification, Greenglass testified, consisted of the side of a box of Jello, a prepared dessert made of gelatine powder. Greenglass testified that Rosenberg cut a V-shaped section out of the side of this Jello box, gave one side to Ruth Greenglass and kept one side for himself.

THE GOVERNMENT'S CASE

1. The first government witness was Max Elitcher, a graduate electrical engineer. Elitcher testified that he was

Ann Sidorovich. Greenglass testified Rosenberg asked him to remember her face because "Julius said this is the woman who he thinks would come out to see us at Albuquerque (where Mrs. Greenglass lived, near Los Alamos) to receive information from myself on the atomic bomb." Greenglass testified Rosenberg that night also established an alternate means of identification between Greenglass and Rosenberg's representative in case Ann Sidorovich was unable to travel. This alternate means of identification, Greenglass testified, consisted of the side of a box of Jello, a prepared dessert made of gelatine powder. Greenglass testified that Rosenberg cut a V-shaped section out of the side of this Jello box, gave one side to Ruth Greenglass and kept one side for himself.

A few nights later, Greenglass testified, Rosenberg drove him to a place on 1st Avenue to a rendezvous with a "Russian" who asked about high explosive lenses, the formula of the curve on the lens, the high-explosive used, and the means of detonation.

3

LEGAL HISTORY

Julius and Ethel Rosenberg were indicted January 31, 1951, charged with conspiring between 1944 and 1950 to commit espionage. With them the Grand Jury indicted David Greenglass, Anatoli Yakovlev a Vice-Consul in the Soviet Consulate at New York, and Morton Sobell.

Greenglass pleaded guilty before the trial started. Yakovlev fled the country in 1946 but is still under indictment. Should he return to America, he would have to stand trial.

In June of 1945, back in Los Alamos, Greenglass testified, he received a visit from a man who said to him "Julius sent me" and then produced one part of the Jello box which Greenglass had last seen in Rosenberg's possession. Greenglass testified that he learned subsequently this man was Harry Gold, who has pleaded guilty to espionage. Greenglass testified he gave Gold sketches of new lens molds, how they were used in experiments and descriptions of these experiments. Greenglass testified Gold gave him $500 in return.

In September 1945, Greenglass again went to New York on furlough. On this occasion, Greenglass testified he gave to Rosenberg a pretty good description of the atom bomb. Greenglass testified he was able to produce this description because in the course of his work at Los Alamos "I came in contact with various people who worked on different parts of the project, and also I worked directly on certain apparatus that went in to the bomb, and I met people who talked of the bombs and how they worked". Greenglass

In June of 1945, back in Los Alamos, Greenglass testified, he received a visit from a man who said to him "Julius sent me" and then produced one part of the Jello box which Greenglass had last seen in Rosenberg's possession. Greenglass testified that he learned subsequently this man was Harry Gold, who has pleaded guilty to espionage. Greenglass testified he gave Gold sketches of new lens molds, how they were used in experiments and descriptions of these experiments. Greenglass testified Gold gave him $500 in return.

ions to leave the country and gave Greenglass three sets of instructions to contact the secretary of the Ambassador of the Soviet Union in Mexico City under the alias "I. Jackson". These instructions also entailed contacting the secretaries of the Ambassador of the Soviet Union in Stockholm - under the statue of Linnus, Greenglass testified - and the Ambassador of the Soviet Union in Czechoslovakia. Greenglass testified he had passport pictures made and gave five sets to Rosenberg. Greenglass said Rosenberg then gave them an additional $4000, wrapped in heavy brown paper. He said he gave this package to his brother-in-law, Louis Abel.

5. The third government witness was Dr. Walter S. Koski, a professor of physical chemistry at John Hopkins University and a consultant in the Brookhaven National Laboratories specializing in nuclear chemistry. Dr. Koski testified that he was engaged in

4

Security Information

34

2

Mrs. Greenglass testified that her husband returned to New York in January 1945, when Rosenberg came to their house and received written information from her husband. She testified that a few nights later they went to the Rosenbergs and met Ann Sidorovich. She testified about the Jello box and said that Rosenberg gave her one of the two portions.

In February 1945, Mrs. Greenglass testified, Rosenberg came to see her one night when her sister, Dorothy Abel, was present. She testified that after a few minutes of conversation, Rosenberg asked Dorothy Abel "to take a book and go into the bathroom because he had something private to discuss."

In June 1945, in Albuquerque, she testified Harry Gold came to their apartment and identified himself by producing his half of the Jello box side. She testified Gold asked her husband for the information and that this information was given to Gold later in the afternoon. She testified Gold gave her husband $500.

a few nights later they went to the Rosenbergs and met Ann Sidorovich. She testified about the Jello box and said that Rosenberg gave her one of the two portions.

In February 1945, Mrs. Greenglass testified, Rosenberg came to see her one night when her sister, Dorothy Abel, was present. She testified that after a few minutes of conversation, Rosenberg asked Dorothy Abel "to take a book and go into the bathroom because he had something private to discuss."

In June 1945, in Albuquerque, she testified Harry Gold came to their apartment and identified himself by producing his half of the Jello box side. She testified Gold asked her husband for the information and that this information was given to Gold later in the afternoon. She testified Gold gave her husband $500.

She testified that in September 1945, they returned to New York, and that her husband gave Rosenberg more information in the Rosenberg apartment.

After her husband's discharge from the Army, she testified, they visited the Rosenbergs apartment from time to time. In that apartment, she said, the Rosenbergs showed her a mahogany console

reports over to Yakovlev. Gold testified his espionage duties were "to obtain information from a number of sources in America and to transfer this information to Yakovlev." He testified he met with his source of information after making contact by means of set recognition signals which always involved a code phrase, plus two parts of some object or piece of paper. He testified he paid some of the people he contacted regularly with money given to him by Yakovlev.

When Fuchs was stationed at Los Alamos, Gold testified, Yakovlev told him to go to Albuquerque. He said Yakovlev also gave him a sheet of paper on which was typed the word "Greenglass", then a number "High Street", then "Albuquerque, New Mexico" and then "Recognition signal. I come from Julius". Gold testified "Yakovlev gave me a piece of cardboard which appeared to have been cut from a package of food of some sort. It was cut in an odd shape and Yakovlev told me that the man Greenglass, would have the matching piece of cardboard. Yakovlev told me just in case the man Greenglass should not be present when I called in Albuquerque, that his wife would have the information and that she would turn it over to me. Yakovlev gave me an envelope which he said contained $500 and told me to give it to Greenglass."

Gold testified he went to Albuquerque, contacted Greenglass, produced his part of the Jello box side, and matched it with the one Greenglass had. He said Greenglass told him to return later in the afternoon. When he did return, Gold said, Greenglass gave him "the material on the atom bomb" and he gave Greenglass the envelope containing $500 which Yakovlev had given him. Gold testified he also received documents from Fuchs on this visit and returned to New York with two envelopes, one marked "Doctor" and one, from Greenglass, marked "Other". He testified he gave both envelopes to Yakovlev back in New York. Two weeks later, he testified, "Yakovlev told me the information which I had given him some two weeks previous had been sent immediately to the Soviet Union". He said that the information which I received from Greenglass was "extremely excellent and very valuable." Gold testified Fuchs subsequently gave him information about the first atomic explosion at Alamogordo, New Mexico, and Gold said he gave this information to Yakovlev.

8. The eighth government witness was Dr. George Bernhardt. He testified that in May 1950, Rosenberg asked him what injections were needed to go to Mexico.

Gold was asked "Does this information that has been read to you, together with the sketch, concern a type of atomic bomb which was actually used by the United States of America?" Gold replied "It does. It is the bomb we dropped at Nagasaki, similar to it."

13. The thirteenth government witness was Manuel Giner de Los Rios, who testified through an interpreter that he met Sobell in Mexico City in July, 1950. He said Sobell asked him how it was possible to leave the country without taking steps in good order. He said Sobell told him he was afraid to return to the United States because he thought military police were looking for him and he would have to go into the Army. Rios testified that there came a time when Sobell left Mexico City to go to Vera Cruz.

14. The fourteenth government witness was Minerva Bravo Espinosa, an employee of a Mexico City oculist. She testified through an interpreter that Sobell purchased a pair of glasses under the alias, Sand.

15. The fifteenth government witness was Jose Broccado Vendrell, a Vera Cruz hotel owner. He identified the hotel regis-

Gold testified he went to Albuquerque, contacted Greenglass, produced his part of the Jello box side, and matched it with the one Greenglass had. He said Greenglass told him to return later in the afternoon. When he did return, Gold said, Greenglass gave him "the material on the atom bomb" and he gave Greenglass the envelope containing $500 which Yakovlev had given him. Gold testified he also received documents from Fuchs on this visit and returned to New York with two envelopes, one marked "Doctor" and one, from Greenglass, marked "Other". He testified he gave both envelopes to Yakovlev back in New York. Two weeks later, he testified, "Yakovlev told me the information which I had given him some two weeks previous had been sent immediately to the Soviet Union". He said that the information which I received from Greenglass was "extremely excellent and very valuable." Gold testified Fuchs subsequently gave him information about the first atomic explosion at Alamogordo, New Mexico, and Gold said he gave this information to Yakovlev.

GREETINGS FROM JULIUS

REDS, JELL-O, & THE POLITICAL LEFT

The Red Scare is one of post-war America's most studied phenomena. Declassified documents play a vital role in written histories of the Red Scare, as scholars unveil the government's excessive response to communists within American borders. At the center of this history of repression stands the trial of Julius and Ethel Rosenberg, a piece of government theater put on as a morality tale for the American Left—do not stray too far from the flock—and an affirmation to middle America that the paranoia about and preoccupation with communism was justified.

Perhaps it is fitting that a food brand so self-consciously American as Jell-O took center stage at the espionage trial of alleged communist spies Julius and Ethel Rosenberg.

The end of the story is crucial to understanding the importance of its beginning: in 1951, both Rosenbergs were found guilty and sentenced to death, a judgment for the crime of espionage unprecedented and unrepeated.

The judge, when handing down the sentence, admonished the Rosenbergs for "a crime worse then murder;" giving away atomic secrets that could potentially harm "millions of innocent people." He then blamed them for the escalation of communist activity in Korea. His comments embrace a butterfly effect-style reasoning—if a spy opens her mouth in one hemisphere, a nuclear bomb goes off in another—more than actual data, but what sounds like hyperbole today was rational judicial reasoning in the Cold War period.

In 1949, four years before the Rosenbergs were executed, the United States discovered the Soviet Union was testing nuclear weapons. The U.S. government assumed it would have taken the Soviets many more years to develop the technology necessary to produce an atomic bomb. Communist backwaters with starving citizens don't have nuclear weapons, right?

The US government led the public to believe that while American nuclear capability is acceptable, other nations such as the Soviet Union could not shoulder the responsibility of nuclear arms. In reality, the US feared impressionable countries with struggling economies would seek to align themselves with the communist nation, who would offer aid and a perceived military might equal to that of the United States, weakening US global influence. So much for containment.

The spread of nuclear capacity among communist nations was a nightmare scenario for the US government, and they needed to reassert their power at home. The US government declared that the Soviet Union

must have stolen the secrets of the atomic bomb. In 1950, Julius and Ethel Rosenberg and a cadre of American chemists and German nuclear physicists were fingered by the US government.

The accusations faced by the Rosenbergs were severe: Julius and Ethel were allegedly at the center of a spy ring that gave key information about the atomic bomb to the Soviet Union. The most important piece of evidence in their trial was a Jell-O box, used to corroborate witness testimonies claiming Julius coordinated meetings between informants and the Soviets.

The Jell-O box, according to two witnesses, was a communication device meant to help Julius' spies identify one another. Julius, the story goes, had cut the box into two parts, giving one to Soviet agent (and US citizen) Harry Gold and the other to David Greenglass, Ethel's brother. When they met, the two men were to show each other the box halves, making sure they fit together, and speak a code phrase. According to the trial

Ethyl and Julius Rosenberg visiting in prison.
(photo by Roger Higgins)

transcript, the phrase was the simple and obvious "greetings from Julius," although the FBI coached Gold on this part of his testimony. Recently declassified transcripts show Gold uttered a different code phrase during secret, pre-trial hearings.

The Jell-O box was the prosecution's most important—and effective—piece of evidence. The prosecution paraded it around, flashing it at the jury and asking witness after witness if the box that the attorney was holding did, in fact, "resemble the box used"—yes, it did "resemble the box used".

The alleged Jell-O box had never been found, perhaps destroyed—being evidence of espionage and all—so the prosecution simply bought another one at the grocery store and cut it in a pattern similar to that described by the state's key witnesses.

It was here that the Rosenbergs fell prey to the recognizability of the all-American brand. For one, Harry Gold—who received thirty years in prison for his part in the spy ring—at first could not name the type of box used, recalling "a torn or cut piece of card" in his first statements to the FBI.

By the trial Gold miraculously remembered what kind of box it was, thanks to David Greenglass, the prosecution's other witness and, conveniently, Gold's cell-block mate. The trial came down to the testimonies of Harry Gold and David Greenglass, both of whom testified the Rosenbergs were at the center of the spy ring.

The Jell-O box was the only piece of material evidence presented by the prosecution, and it, of course, was fabricated.

The most confounding thing about the trial is the fact that neither Julius nor Ethel ever confessed to anything. They wouldn't even confess to being communists. After all of their appeals had been denied, both Rosenbergs were offered a commuted sentence—meaning they would not be executed—in exchange for a confession. But they refused, claiming until their deaths that they had been framed by the government.

Because they never confessed, and because the material evidence in their trial was fabricated and oral testimony was likely coached, coerced, or unreliable (Harry Gold was notorious for conjuring up complicated fantasies), many people — most notably the Rosenbergs' two sons—believe Julius and Ethel's story that they were set up as part of a government public relations campaign.

This campaign was meant to reassure American citizens of the US's ability to ferret out communist spies and at the same time let them know they could feel good about America's exceptional commitment to hold a fair trial, even in the face of such obvious monsters as communist spies.

The Red Scare needed show trials, blacklists, hearings—public spectacles transmitted into homes, publicly shaming American citizens for their political beliefs—to reassure the country that the fight against communism was real, and worth all of the expensive military programs and questionable foreign policies.

We must remember that while accusing the innocent marks everyone as a potential target, attacking actual Leftists unmakes political activity and intellectualism, sewing seeds of fear and distrust into Leftist communities. The louder the government spoke against communism, the more difficult—or risky—it became for citizens to speak.

To say the 1950s were quiet years lacking in dissent would be a mischaracterization, falling prey to mediated images of nuclear families and uncomfortable marriages. The Left was alive, it always is. Resistance is ever present. But the climate of fear and the publicity of punishment surrounding the Rosenbergs' trial and execution froze the Left out of political life.

Liberals and other progressives in government went along with the effort so as not to seem disloyal; the trial disarmed a generation of activists. The Rosenbergs' case remains salient because it was scary—Leftists found they lived in a country where communists were put to death.

Yes, it is possible the Rosenbergs committed some level of espionage. But their sentence was extreme and, as stated above, unprecedented. Guilt or innocence is not what we are after here. The Rosenbergs have become as iconic as the Jell-O used to incriminate them, and their story is told time and again because it is a complicated one that does not lend itself to black and white moralizing.

Leftists should be as unsure of their guilt as they are certain that the trial was used to deploy public sentiment against the left.

PARIS: JUNE 1953

Paris, along with much of Europe, exploded into protests after the United States government executed Julius and Ethel Rosenberg. In Paris, over a thousand people were arrested and several were murdered after police opened fire on the crowds.

The images above are of protests in Paris against the Rosenbergs' imprisonment and execution.

TO CATCH A SPY

All of the documents in this book were once classified, which means only government agents with security clearances could read them. But what happens when someone with a security clearance defects and decides to spy for the other side?

Is it possible to know who will defect, and why? Could you pick them out of a crowd? According to a 2008 report commissioned by the Department of Defense, 173 people have defected and committed espionage against the US since 1947.

Reasons include money, disgruntlement, coercion, and, of course, good old fashioned thrill-seeking. The report thoroughly profiles spies and we used the data to create the mock document below so YOU have the tools you need to catch a spy.

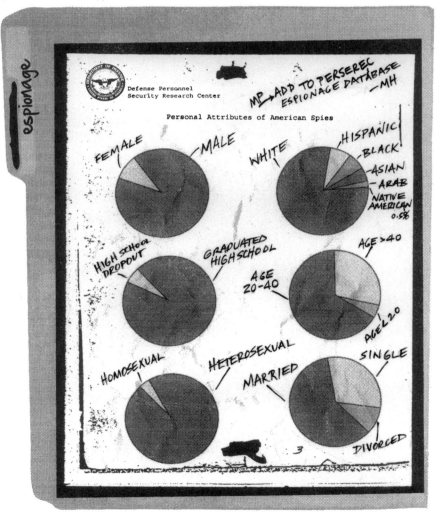

DIY EVIDENCE

Follow the government's lead and fabricate your own evidence. Show the defense who's boss by parading these two box halves up and down the jury box. Or use them to set-up secret rendezvous for your covert missions. Hours of fun with your friends!

RECOMMENDED READING:

Secret Agents: The Rosenberg Case, McCarthyism, & Fifties America
by Marjorie Garber and Rebecca L. Walkowitz, eds. (New York, NY: Routledge, 1995)

Final Verdict: What Really Happened in the Rosenberg Case
by Walter Schneir (New York, NY: Melville House, 2010)

*The Rosenberg Letters: A Complete Edition of the Prison Correspondence of
Julius and Ethel Rosenberg*
Edited by Michael Meeropol (New York, NY: Routledge, 1994)

Age of McCarthyism: A Brief History with Documents
by Ellen Schrecker (Bostom, MA: Bedford Books of St. Martin's Press, 1994)

SECRET 4
CASTRO
MILKSHAKE

⸐DOCUMENT

Presented here are excerpts from a transcript of a secret meeting between Fidel Castro, President of Cuba, and Peter Tarnoff, of the US Department of State. The primary purpose of the meeting was to negotiate the release of political prisoners by Cuba and the United States. Castro and Tarnoff reached an agreement that was announced publicly several days later. However, this secret meeting was never reported. The meeting and transcript remained secret until 2002.

In the excerpts presented here, Castro describes assassination attempts coordinated and funded by the CIA.

SECRET

MEMORANDUM OF CONVERSATION

Participants:

US side

Peter Tarnoff, Executive Secretary, Department of State
Robert Pastor, National Security Council Staff
Stephanie van Reigersberg, Interpreter/Notetaker

Cuban side

Fidel Castro Ruz, President
Jose Millar, Executive Secretary,Office of the Presidency, Notetaker
Juanita Vera, Interpreter

(Received by Jose A. Naranjo, Special Assistant to the President
and Minister of the Food Industry)

Date/Time/Place: December 3-4, 1978; 10:00 p.m. - 3:00 a.m.
                   Palace of the Revolution, Havana Cuba

Subject: US/Cuban relations

Castro: So, how was Varadero?

Tarnoff: We had a delightful day following our talks with the
Vice President -- we had a very good time.

SECRET

NSC NLC-17-008. XDS-3 12/8/98 (Tarnoff, Peter)
-5/9/02-

Castro:

    There are other things I could add. One thing we
discovered recently that happened during the Carter
Administration was an attempt on my life carried out
by the CIA while I was in Jamaica. This was not Kennedy
or Johnson, but the Carter Administration. I will limit
myself to mentioning these things.

Castro: I am sorry if I don't answer your points in the same
order, I am not even going to try. First, on Jamaica. I am
not blaming President Carter. I ratify my impression that
Carter is not a man who would plan, authorize, or instigate
attempts against the lives of other leaders. I repeat I
think Carter is incapable of that, and in all honesty I
would say so publicly. But although he is not the author
of this, it did happen during the Carter Administration.
If you wish I will give you all the information we have on
it, although it was a public occurrence. I can understand,
Mr. Tarnoff, that you don't have time to see everything
that is printed but it was published in the Jamaican press.
The Jamaican authorities said that the person responsible
was a Jamaican who was contacted by the CIA in Canada, was
trained by the CIA and confessed publicly. This much is
obvious -- he worked for the CIA and he was involved in an
attempt against my life. All of this gives us some idea of the
chaos and anarchy which prevails in U.S. Government institutions.
But I am not charging Carter, and I say this most sincerely.
Don't imagine that we are developing an assassination psychosis.
We are used to it and it does not worry us.
We just mentioned it as an example. But it is one which no
doubt did occur and we would say so publicly. I can try to
get the information for you and perhaps you could ask the
Jamaican Government to find out more.

Castro: I was informed that a statement was made by a
Jamaican citizen who had been contacted by the CIA to make
an attempt on my life. You asked me why I believe it. I
have 20 years of experience in assessing news. The case
was quite strange but I saw no need to doubt the confession.
Perhaps it was false but I did believe it. Why? We have
a lot of background on assassination attempts. We have seen
them many times and we understand the CIA and know how it
operates.

SECRET

-33-

Castro: Yes, you are right. The problem with these re-
leases is that we do not know how dangerous these people
still are. Some were guilty of assassination attempts.
Izaguirre, and Paulita Grau who brought poison for me from
the United States, both were imprisoned for attempts on

-34-

my life. Paulita Grau brought poison which she gave to a
man in a cafeteria. I went to that cafeteria and ordered
a chocolate milkshake. The man had put the pellet in the
refrigerator and it froze I think. Anyway, he got nervous
and didn't drop it in. I drank that milkshake, and she is
in the United States now.

Tarnoff: We are aware of that.

Castro: By the way, no Cuban in the United States knows
that you have been here. No one at all knows. I beg you
not to put us on the spot. You could place us in a very
embarrassing position.

Tarnoff: We are taking the same precautions. But if we
think that there has been any unauthorized leak, we will
let you know immediately.

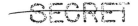

WE ARE
AWARE OF THAT
THE CIA'S SECRET PROGRAM
TO ASSASSINATE FIDEL CASTRO

Fidel Castro was almost killed by a chocolate milkshake. With over 600 attempts to assassinate the revolutionary communist leader with knives, guns, and bombs, the closest the United States government came to taking him down was when they tried poisoning his favorite food, chocolate milkshakes.

During the 1960s and 1970s, Fidel Castro enjoyed a creamy chocolate milkshake every afternoon at the Havana Libre Hotel. Tourists would gather everyday in the hotel's dining room and lobby to gawk at and snap pictures of the notorious leader enjoying his afternoon snack, and to this day the hotel regales its visitors with the tale of the closest attempt ever on Castro's life.

The United States government knew Castro's love of milkshakes was reliably habitual and sought to exploit it. The CIA hired a Cuban ex-patriot living in the United States—a woman opposed to the communist government—to use CIA-mafia connections to get a cyanide capsule to Cuba.

At the time, the mafia was reliable transportation because they traded goods from the United States to Cuba, something more legitimate businesses were prevented from doing by the US government's trade embargo. Because they had controlled much of the tourist industries before the revolution forced them out, the mafia was sympathetic to the woman's mission and helped her get the cyanide to Cuba.

Once in Cuba, the CIA-hired assassin connected with anti-Castro rebels, who introduced her to a sympathetic kitchen worker at the Havana Libre Hotel. Little is known about this kitchen worker—his age, current whereabouts, and even his side of the story have gone unrecorded, leaving it to Castro and the US government to argue about what really happened.

According to the US government, the brave kitchen worker fully intended to dose the dictator's chocolate dessert with cyanide. But it had been stored in the freezer and had frozen to the metal tray—crumbling when the worker tried to grab it.

Castro boasts that he not only knew the CIA's hired assassin was on the island to poison his chocolate milkshake, but even knew which day the kitchen worker intended to dose his shake with cyanide. And he drank it anyway.

He claims he knew the kitchen worker would never have the audacity to assassinate him, Fidel Castro, Prime Minister and First Secretary of the Communist Party of Cuba. And potentially, he was right. There is no evidence which tale—Castro's or the CIA's—is more correct.

While the U.S. government has released documents that mention attempts on Castro's life, such as the one presented here and the recently redacted collection of CIA documents called the "Family Jewels" — nearly 700 pages of declassified documents detailing some of the more nefarious CIA projects (such as MKULTRA, see chapter 5)—they generally try to keep assassination attempts a

Venezuelan President Hugo Chavez enjoying a milkshake with Fidel Castro while Fidel was in the hospital. August 2006.

secret and all memoranda, directives, and executive orders to assassinate Castro have been destroyed.

A 1967 CIA "eyes only" memorandum in a "report on plots to assassinate Fidel Castro" explained why there are no documents giving proof of this program:

> Because of the extreme sensitivity of the operations being discussed or attempted, as a matter of principle no official records were kept of planning, of approvals, or of implementation. The few written records that do exist are either largely tangential to the main events or were put on paper from memory years afterward. (25 April 1967 CIA eyes only memorandum; see excerpt below).

As you can see, the document published in this chapter can be described as "largely tangential"—Castro and the Pentagon meet, and end up in an unplanned-for discussion on the CIA's assassination attempt. In the absence of official CIA records, this document stands as one of the only records of the poisoned milkshake.

Castro, unlike the CIA, loves to tell the story, as does even the Havana Libre Hotel—repeating Castro's version of events. This assassination

SECRET—EYES ONLY

25 April 1967

MEMORANDUM

This reconstruction of Agency involvement in plans to assassinate Fidel Castro is at best an imperfect history. Because of the extreme sensitivity of the operations being discussed or attempted, as a matter of principle no official records were kept of planning, of approvals, or of implementation. The few written records that do exist are either largely tangential to the main events or were put on paper from memory years afterward.

Excerpt from the 1967 CIA Inspector General's "Report On Plots To Assassinate Fidel Castro."

CYANIDE

Cyanide is an age-old poison. Thousands of years ago Romans and Egyptians distilled peach pits to make cyanide, knowing somehow that the fruit contains small amounts of the poison in its seeds. As a poison, cyanide works by making your body unable to use oxygen.

In smaller amounts, however, it is used in many commercial products: vitamins, jewelry, adhesives, computer electronics, fire retardants, airplane brakes, cosmetics, dyes, nylon, nail polish remover, paints, pharmaceuticals, Plexiglas, rocket propellant, and table salt.

---

attempt has attained the status of legend, a tale Castro constantly retells not only to prove his own virility and legitimacy as a leader, but as a metaphor for the resiliency of Cuba in the face of a U.S. government preoccupied by the communists to the south.

But if Castro had not happened to mention it in this secret meeting, would we believe the fantastical tale of the poisoned milkshake? It's almost too silly to believe. Would it seem a tall tale invented so Castro could revel in the frustration of the U.S. government, whose containment policy had failed?

The poisoned milkshake is but one of the hundreds of attempts on Fidel Castro's life from the Cuban revolution in 1959 to the present day. Although in 1976 President Gerald Ford made it illegal for any arm of the U.S. government to make attempts on the life of a foreign leader, writer Fabian Escalante has documented assassination attempts through the most recent Bush administration.

Attempts on Castro's life range from frightening examples of CIA violence to comical cartoon villainy. They have tried to shoot, bomb, stab, and poison him; they have also tried to make his hair fall out, explode his cigar, booby trap a conch shell, and dose his wetsuit with LSD.

Without government secrecy, these assassination attempts would not be possible. Many Americans believe in a doctrine called American exceptionalism—the idea that the U.S. occupies a special position as a world leader and has a responsibility to influence world politics, which sometimes can mean acting extra-legally in order to spread democracy, contain communism, and murder leaders who threaten global capitalism.

For people who believe in American exceptionalism, government secrecy is a "necessary evil," something that enables the United States to maintain its position as world leader (and the President's popular moniker "leader of the Free World"). Enabled by the doctrine of American exceptionalism, U.S. government secrecy is so extensive that its public policy of nonengagement with Cuba had no bearing on reality whatsoever.

The U.S. met regularly with Castro. Our document shows a meeting between Castro and the Pentagon during which they struck a deal for the trade of political prisoners for Cuban exiles, a deal that was publicly attributed to a Cuban-American exile group.

The U.S. government was meeting with Castro, and they were attempting to assassinate him. But the U.S. public knew of none of this.

Fidel Castro escorted by the NYPD after an assassination attempt in New York City. 24 April 1959.

THE FIRST 150 ATTEMPTS TO ASSASSINATE FIDEL CASTRO

The United States has been involved in the planning of "638 Ways to Kill Fidel Castro," according to a 2007 BBC documentary of that name. The graph below lays out the first 150 assassination plots for which arrests were made or evidence exists. Each symbol represents one planned assassination attempt, and the type of plot it was. No word yet on whether the CIA has realized "I almost died of embarrassment" is just an expression.

LEGEND

SHARP SHOOTER	POISON
AMBUSH	UNSPECIFIED
PLANTED BOMB	STAB
LAUNCHED BOMB	MELTED ALIVE
	EMBARRASSMENT

FOOD INVOLVED

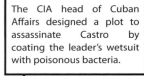

The CIA head of Cuban Affairs designed a plot to assassinate Castro by coating the leader's wetsuit with poisonous bacteria.

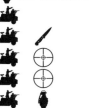

Employees at a steel mill planned to push Castro into a vat of melted iron while he was touring the facility.

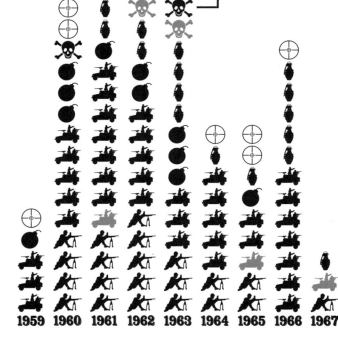

1959 1960 1961 1962 1963 1964 1965 1966 1967 1968 1969 1970 1971

CAN YOU MATCH THE CONTROVERSIAL LEADER WITH HIS FAVORITE FOOD ?

Fidel Castro isn't the only globally hated (or loved) leader with a favorite food. Test your culinary dictator knowledge with this quiz:

 BIN LADEN

 STALIN

 MAO

 HITLER

 KHOMEINI

 BUSH

 MUSSOLINI

HONEY ON TOAST

PORK

GRAPES

BREAD AND WATER

MEAT

NOUGAT

TACOS

57

Answers: Bin Laden loves bread and water. Stalin loves meat. Mao loves pork. Hitler loves honey on toast. Khomeini loves nougat. Bush loves tacos. Mussolini loves grapes.

THE TOP 5 ~~CIA ASSASSINATION PLOTS~~ PRANKS! ON FIDEL CASTRO

1 POISONED CIGARS

Known to enjoy a smoke or two, El Comandante Fidel narrowly avoided years of poisoned cigars. The CIA has, on numerous occasions, tried to slip cigars packed with poison into Fidel's private supply. Unfortunately for the Agency, Fidel quit smoking in 1985. Apparently it can be bad for your health.

2 HAIRLESS CASTRO

In 1960 Fidel came to New York City to address the General Assembly of the United Nations. With him under their nose, the CIA just couldn't resist. The CIA attempted to put thallium salt in his shoes. Also known as "The Poisoner's Poison," thallium salt won't just kill you, it will make you lose all your hair. The CIA was hoping for a double whammy: embarrassment before death.

3 GET HIM SUPERHIGH

When the thallium salt plot didn't pan out, the CIA didn't give up. Knowing Fidel would be addressing the UN and holding various televised interviews, the boys at the Agency thought they'd get him super high. The CIA infused a cigar with LSD and tried to slip it in with Fidel's private stash. Cuban Security Services claim the plot didn't work, while Fidel swears the UN is the most beautiful, colorful place he's ever been.

4 EXPLODING SEA SHELL

When not enjoying a good cigar or milkshake, Fidel loves to go underwater fishing. The CIA, again, hoped to ruin the things Fidel loves by trying to kill him. This time, they put together a plan to plant seashells with explosives at his favorite fishing site. The CIA chose some exotic and colorful shells hoping to draw Fidel's attention. Fidel didn't fall for it. Maybe they should have slipped him some LSD first; "Whoa, I gotta have that shell, it looks just like Che!"

5 BASEBALL BOMB

Undeterred by plots to kill him, Fidel returned to New York City in 1979 to again address the UN General Assembly. Equally undeterred by years of unsuccessful attempts to assassinate Fidel, the CIA again couldn't resist having the Cuban leader under their noses. This time the CIA planned to pack some baseballs with contact explosives and throw them at Fidel's motorcade.

HONORABLE MENTION

Those jokesters at the CIA have a seemingly never ending supply of pranks. They've tried planting a gun in a video camera that was to film Fidel. They've tried poisoning his Chinese Food. They've even plotted to murder his friends, so they could assassinate him at their funeral.... "Gotcha!" Those agency boys are hilarious.

RECOMMENDED READING:

Executive Action: 634 Ways to Kill Fidel Castro
by Fabián Escalante (New York, NY: Ocean Press, 2006)

The Prison Letters of Fidel Castro
by Fidel Castro with an introduction by Ann Louise Bardach (New York, NY: Nation Books, 1959)

Without Fidel: A Death Foretold in Miami, Havana, and Washington
by Ann Louise Bardach (New York, NY: Scribner, 2009)

SECRET CIA POPCORN 5

THE DOCUMENT

This report was originally published in the CIA's internal journal *Studies in Intelligence*. In it, the author tries to determine whether subliminal messaging would be an effective tactic for the intelligence community. The original report is excerpted here for the sake of brevity.

TITLE: The Operational Potential Of Subliminal Perception

AUTHOR: Richard Gafford

VOLUME: 2   ISSUE: Spring   YEAR: 1958

THE OPERATIONAL POTENTIAL OF
SUBLIMINAL PERCEPTION

Richard Gafford

Perception is demonstrated to have occurred below the threshold of conscious sensory experience when a person responds to a stimulus too weak in intensity or too short in duration for him to be aware of it. Individual behavior without awareness of the stimulus, of which subliminal perception is a subtype, has been a subject of study in psychological laboratories for at least 70 years, and a great deal of technical data has been collected on the subject. Recently it has been associated with some theories of depth analysis and popularized for possible commercial exploitation by the advertising world.

In the most sensational of these popularized experiments, an increase in popcorn sales in a New Jersey movie theater is said to have been stimulated by subliminal interruptions of the feature film with an advertisement urging the patrons to buy popcorn. The exposure time used, a small fraction of a second, was too brief for conscious discrimination by an observer absorbed in the film story but presumably long enough to have some stimulating effect. The advertising men who are currently interested in this phenomenon as a sales technique argue that the short-duration stimulus appeals to a positive motive, for example an appetite for popcorn, without arousing the rational, conscious sales-resistance of the individual, based perhaps on the desire to save money or lose weight.

There are four principal categories of behavior without awareness.

The individual may be unaware of:

a) his behavior itself.

He may be whispering without realizing he is whispering, or he may be moving into a trap without knowing that

---

the trap is there. A special case here is abnormal behavior in which the individual fails to realize what he is doing because his normal awareness and self-control have been interrupted by disturbing agents such as fear, anxiety, illness, drugs, or hypnotic suggestion.

b) the relation of his behavior to some stimulus.

The individual may be unaware of the fact that his interrogator is influencing him by saying "Right" after certain statements and by remaining noncommittal after others. The process called "operant conditioning" falls into this category.

c) the stimulus itself, because of its slight impact.

The individual may be unaware of a very faint sound or a quick flash of light, unaware in the sense that he lacks the usual visual sensations. Subliminal perception falls into this category.

d) the precise nature of the stimulus, as well as its relation to his behavior, because of inattention.

The individual may be aware of vague sensations, but he is not aware either of the source or of the significant content of the stimulation, although his behavior may change in accordance with changes in the stimulus. This category includes a great deal of perceptual activity affecting ordinary social behavior. A person is often unaware of the specific cues and clues to which he is reacting not because the stimulus is insufficient to reach the consciousness but because the effort to be fully aware of all the cues all the time would create too great a cognitive strain.

In persuading a person to do something he normally or rationally would resist doing an intelligence operative can make use of any one of these categories of psychological processes. Usually the purpose is to produce *behavior* of which the individual is unaware. The use of subliminal perception, on the other hand, is a device to keep him unaware of the *source* of his stimulation. The desire here is not to keep him unaware of what he is doing, but rather to keep him unaware of why he is doing it, by masking the external cue or message with subliminal presentation and so stimulating an unrecognized motive.

BEHAVIOR WITHOUT AWARENESS
MKULTRA AND THE CIA'S LEGACY OF
TORTURE AND HUMAN EXPERIMENTATION

At first, this document seemed funny. We chuckled, picturing CIA agents, members of an elite espionage force, dutifully taking notes on the effects of subliminal messages—a technology best known for its connections to science fiction and pop culture.

And really, the conclusion reached by the report's writer—that the human mind is too complex, and rational decision-making far too advanced, to be influenced by a single image frame flashed onto a screen—is a rather obvious one. But then we asked ourselves, for what "operations" would subliminal messaging possibly have been effective? Why was the CIA interested in a technology that induced "behavior without awareness"?

Through our research, we came to understand that subliminal messaging was a brief CIA research interest, undertaken as part of a large CIA project called MKUltra. From 1953 to 1964, CIA agents under MKUltra, along with contracted doctors and scientists, researched and developed mind control technologies and interrogation tactics, using complex psychological experiments to test the limits of human control.

Eventually, the program was disbanded and the majority of its records destroyed, but its effects continue today, for MKUltra scientists developed the sophisticated torture techniques now used around the world by American interrogators.

Subliminal messaging was first publicized by an advertising executive named James Vicary, a wannabe inventor who faked his research on the effects of subliminal messages to get attention for his fast projection machine. In 1957, Vicary held a press conference for this machine, which spliced frames into movies for a fraction of a second, too quick to be recognized by the conscious mind.

He theorized gut instincts would take over, and the associated craving for whatever was being advertised—in his experiments, popcorn and Coca-Cola—would overwhelm rationale. Almost as soon as the story went out on the wires, television networks banned the practice on their airwaves, the Federal Communications Commission looked into a total prohibition, and a Michigan Senator stormed the halls of Congress seeking to make the technology completely illegal. Subliminal messages produced a panicked fear that the Orwellian nightmare of Big Brother had finally come to pass.

The public was afraid of what might happen if subliminal messaging technology got into the wrong hands; in 1957, advertising agencies and the Soviet Union topped the list.

After all, in 1957 Americans were not yet barraged by a constant stream of behavioral profiling ads on the internet. Most importantly, the Cold War colored everything with the threat of Red. But what the fearful

American public did not imagine is that the US government would test the technology for their own purposes, potentially to control foreign spies—or American citizens.

From the report we have, it is unclear whom the government wanted to control. What we do know is that as Senators balked at the practice, the CIA picked up the scent and began researching the technology as part of the MKUltra program.

Many CIA programs are kept secret from Congress, and even occasionally from the President; the MKUltra program was one of the most secretive and controversial CIA initiatives ever uncovered. For over a decade, the CIA enlisted the help of hundreds of scientists to study the effects of LSD, PCP, barbiturates, sensory deprivation, and electroshock on the minds of subjects both witting and unwitting. Prisoners and patients at mental hospitals were tested on not only against their wills, but without their knowledge.

The CIA wanted the power to compel an uncooperative prisoner under interrogation to provide truthful information to the US government. The

THE BLACK BUDGET

Every year Congress approves a black budget. This budget is money appropriated for secret programs and projects Congress knows little or nothing about because they are classified. In 2008 the black budget was a staggering $57.5 billion. Presented here is a comparison of the 2008 US black budget with the entire annual military budgets of Russia, Brazil, and Israel.

UNITED STATES OF AMERICA'S BLACK BUDGET

RUSSIAN MILITARY BUDGET

BRAZILIAN MILITARY BUDGET

ISRAELI MILITARY BUDGET

information needed to be reliable, so the search for truth serums and personality reprogramming—so-called "psychic driving"—began.

The MKUltra program's research was based entirely on the development of interrogation tactics, although ostensibly the tactics were being researched so American troops would be better prepared if they came across them in Soviet interrogation chambers.

Survivors are still coming forward to talk about their harrowing experiences at the hands of government-sponsored scientists. Some do not remember being drugged with LSD, given electroshock therapy or put into comas with large doses of insulin, but nevertheless they are still reeling from the medical effects of such extreme manipulation of brain physiology.

Naomi Klein, in her book *The Shock Doctrine*, has a particularly compelling account of a woman who, in her early 20s, was subjected to hundreds of electroshock treatments as part of MKUltra experiments in creating more compliant prisoners.

Not all patients were tested on against their will, though; some were students at prestigious universities who volunteered for the studies. Ted Kaczynski, better known as the Unabomber, was one such student. While studying at Harvard, he was an LSD test subject.

LSD, Angel Dust, electroshock, hypnosis, uppers, downers, "magicians' arts" (a phrase actually used in a government report)—nothing was too extreme to be tested by the CIA. It is easy to get caught up in the far-fetched, and occasionally bizarre, mind control techniques studied in the MKUltra program.

Mind control and brainwashing are sensational fodder for pop culture and conspiracy theories. But two journalists, Naomi Klein and Alfred McCoy, remind us that perhaps the most insidious and enduring legacy of MKUltra are the torture techniques used by American interrogators today.

Klein and McCoy's work concentrates on MKUltra's legacy, a body of knowledge about the human capacity for pain, humiliation and isolation. One of the tactics developed by CIA-sponsored scientists, they explain, was sensory deprivation.

The goal of sensory deprivation is to completely disorient the prisoner from his sense of self. Divorced from the ability to see, hear ambient noise, or to feel even his own body in space—gloved hands and arms prevent it—a prisoner will become susceptible to suggestion and more compliant. After only a few days, psychosis sets in. Sensory deprivation goes beyond solitary confinement; it is a state of being in which even a prisoner's sense of time and place are completely removed. Sensory deprivation is torture and can certainly cause behavior without awareness.

Sensory deprivation, subliminal messages and LSD testing are historically tied to the photographs, released in 2004, depicting American soldiers torturing prisoner's at Abu Ghraib prison in Iraq. Some of these pictures have become iconic in the most horrid of ways.

A hooded prisoner, standing on a small box with arms outstretched, electric wires attached to his hands. A soldier smiling and giving the thumbs up next to a row of detainees, all completely naked save for the hoods covering their heads.

MKUltra was designed, explicitly, to replicate the possible scenarios that might be encountered by Americans being detained and interrogated oversees, specifically in the Soviet Union. By design, MKUltra applied scientific methods—however dubious—to the experience of torture, enabling them to calculate how drug combinations, hours spent in sensory deprivation chambers, and physical pain would make prisoners susceptible to the suggestions of their interrogators.

MKUltra's science of torture was not only used to train Americans to resist these techniques in the field, but is directly employed by Americans in oversees prisons. There are photos and declassified memos as evidence, and abuse of prisoners continues to be uncovered by the media. Many suggest that these techniques have made American soldiers less safe by proving to the rest of the world that the country has little respect for human life and dignity.

When MKUltra's documents were released in 1975, World War II was a reality understood by all adults. In undertaking these experiments, the United States spat in the face of the Nuremberg codes protecting human subjects, and the 1949 Geneva Conventions on torture, both of which were developed after the Nazis' torturous medical experiments on concentration camp prisoners were revealed.

Nazi experiments, if you can call them that, included testing hallucinogens, an experiment the United States directly replicated under the MKUltra program. Any notion of human rights and international solidarity against torture and the wholesale degradation of people was summarily pushed aside in favor of Cold War extremism and a complete disregard for human dignity.

Experimentation on unwitting subjects ostensibly ended in 1964, when the MKUltra program's directors felt the project had run its course and 1960s activists were changing the political climate. But the torture continues, using techniques developed under MKUltra.

Subliminal messages have become nothing more than a pop culture phenomenon, and most people are unaware that the CIA was ever interested in them as a mind control tactic. It is important to be aware, however, of how the U.S.'s Cold War foreign policy was used to justify a range of experiments, espionage against the American Left, and, of course, wars.

The legacy of these mind control and torture experiments continues today, hindered only by the public's outraged response.

5 DRUGS TESTED BY THE CIA FOR MIND CONTROL

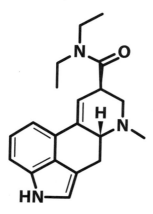

1 L.S.D.

From 1954-1963 the CIA tested the brain-washing capabilities of LSD under the aptly titled Operation Midnight Climax. The CIA *ran a brothel* in San Francisco where prostitutes doubled as temporary agents, slipping LSD into the drinks of unsuspecting johns so the Agency could study the effects of the drug as a potential truth serum. CIA Agents stayed up all night watching the encounters through two-way mirrors and hidden cameras.

2 MESCALINE

In 1953 tennis pro Harold Blauer died from a mescaline overdose administered to him at the New York State Psychiatric Institute. Blauer was suffering from depression and had checked himself into the hospital. He then unknowingly became a test subject of the CIA funded Project Pelican; an MKUltra program testing potential uses of mescaline. The circumstances behind Blauer's death stayed covered up until 1987.

3 CANNABIS

In 1943 the CIA predecessor organization OSS tested cannabis as a truth serum on August Del Gracio, a New York City mobster who worked for "Lucky" Luciano. After getting way too high and falling asleep, Del Gracio proceeded to spill the beans about the inner-workings of the mob. However, future tests proved more successful at instigating the munchies then procuring any hidden secrets.

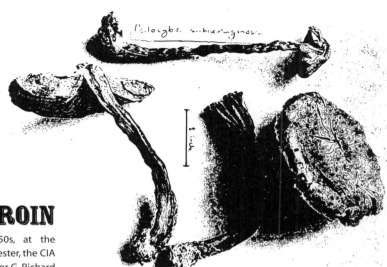

Psilocybe subaeruginosa

1 inch

4 HEROIN

In the early 1950s, at the University of Rochester, the CIA contracted Professor G. Richard Wendt to test heroin as a potential truth serum, which he did on both his students and himself. His research led to the horrific and obvious conclusion that forcing heroin addiction on prisoners and then refusing to give it to them would be an effective truth serum. The stress from the withdrawal would be so great that interrogators would be able to coerce information from prisoners by promising them the drug. Wendt himself refused to experience this withdrawal completely, remaining addicted to heroin until his death in 1977.

5 'SHROOMS

Having heard ancient tales of mushrooms with magic powers, including the procurement of truth, the CIA underwrote a series of expeditions to Mexico in the 1950s to track down what is now colloquially referred to as shrooms. Thousands of dollars later the CIA had brought shrooms to the Western world, but were no closer to the truth.

AND THE WINNER IS

The CIA never came close to finding the magical compound that could brain-wash an individual, but it wasn't due to a lack of trying. The CIA spent nearly two decades developing and purifying LSD with the pharmaceutical company Eli Lilly and testing the synthesized mixture on thousands of participants, willing and unwilling. Sadly and unsurprisingly, willing participants were sought and found on college campuses, while prisoners, mental patients, and people of color were tested on without their knowledge.

JUDAS PRIEST, THE UNABOMBER, AND A CIA AGENT WALK INTO A BAR...
A BRIEF ECOLOGY OF MIND CONTROL

SUBLIMINAL MIND CONTROL

In late 1957 James Vicary held a press conference announcing success with subliminal mind control. Using the tachistoscope to flash imperceptible messages on the screen of a New Jersey movie theater, Vicary claimed to have convinced the audience they were hungry and should "eat popcorn."

The experiment proved to be a failure. Total mind control through subliminal messages is a hoax.

Vicary's invention created a media frenzy.
SUBLIMINAL MESSAGES
became a pop culture phenomenon.

The Beatles injected subliminal messages into popular music with the 1966 album *Revolver*, after John Lennon stumbled upon the recording technique of
BACKMASKING;
the deliberate playing of a sound or message backward in a recording. The Beatles used it to mass effect with their hidden message "Paul is dead."

The Beatles' subliminal messages had tremendous influence over
CHARLES MANSON.
Chuck believed the Beatles were speaking to him about the coming race war in the hidden messages of Revolution #9.

JUDAS PRIEST
released the album *Stained Class* in 1978. It would come under fire seven years later for containing the subliminal message "do it" in the song *Better By You, Better Than Me.*

In 1985 two boys listened to the Judas Priest album *Stained Class* and then committed
SUICIDE.

After James Vance and Ray Belknap commited suicide, their familes sued Judas Priest claiming subliminal messages on the album *Stained Class* were to blame. In his decision allowing the case to proceed, Judge Whitehead referenced Vicary's popcorn experiments from 1957.

CENTRAL INTELLEGENCE AGENCY

In 1958 the CIA thoroughly researched and then recreated Vicary's subliminal message experiment in a Virginia movie theater.

During the early 1960s LSD was tested by the CIA with participant consent at universities, including **HARVARD.**

UNABOMBER

Ted Kaczynski was a Harvard undergraduate and MKULTRA LSD test subject in the early 1960s.

During the 1950s and 60s the CIA conducted and funded experiments seeking total human mind control under the code-named program **MKULTRA.** Among them were experiments with subliminal messaging.

ABU GHRAIB

In 2004 pictures were unearthed showing torture and abuse by the US government of prisoners at the Abu Ghraib prison in Iraq. A direct lineage to the mind control research and experiments of MKULTRA can be, and has been, traced.

LSD

During the 1950s and 60s the CIA researched, refined, and extensively tested the drug LSD under the MKULTRA program.

During the Iraq War, at detention centers and prisons like Abu Ghraib, the US used, and continues to use, music as a tool in torture interrogations.

PRINCE, EMINEM & TUPAC

Aside from one-word names and failed aliases, these artists share two other things in common: 1. Each has used subliminal messages in their music and 2. The US government has used each artist's music as a tool in torture interrogations.

A week after being secretly dosed with LSD by a CIA agent, Frank Olson committed **SUICIDE.**

The CIA tested LSD on hundreds of people WITHOUT consent, including their own. In 1953 the OK was given to covertly dose Army Scientist Frank Olson.

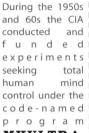

RECOMMENDED READING:

The Shock Doctrine: The Rise of Disaster Capitalism
by Naomi Klein (New York, NY: Picador USA, 2007)

A Question of Torture: CIA Interrogation, from the Cold War to the War on Terror
by Alfred W. McCoy (New York, NY: Metropolitan Books, 2006)

The Search for the "Manchurian Candidate": The CIA and Mid Control: The Secret History of Behavoral Sciences
by John D. Marks (New York, NY: W.W. Norton & Company, Inc, 1979)

Brainwash: The Secret History of Mind Control
by Dominic Streatfeild (New York, NY: Picador, 2007)

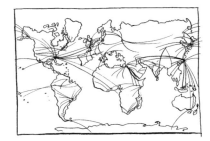

~~CONFIDENTIAL~~ 6
COCA-COLA
LIAISON

ᴛʜᴇDOCUMENT

This declassified memo recounts a meeting held between the vice president of Coca-Cola, former Georgia governor Carl Sanders, and a staff member of the office of National Security Affairs, headed by arch-capitalist Walt W. Rostow. Coca-Cola went to the US government for help in solving an international crisis of their brand:

MEMORANDUM

2926

THE WHITE HOUSE

WASHINGTON

97

~~CONFIDENTIAL~~

February 28, 1967

On Feb 27 reported to Sanders + to and. Kamel that USG had sent telegram.

MEMORANDUM FOR MR. ROSTOW

SUBJECT: Discussion with ex-Governor Carl Sanders and
B. H. Oehlert, Jr., Senior Vice President,
Coca Cola, on February 22, 1967

Sanders explained his proposed mission to Cairo. He wants to discuss with Nasser the advantages to the UAR of not implementing the boycott against .

He will point out that the only thing Coca Cola did in Israel was to agree to sell concentrate to a group of Israeli interests who will be investing their money in a bottling plant for distributing Coca Cola to the small Israeli market. Coca Cola came to this decision only after great pressure mounted by friends of Israel through Jewish grocery stores and soft drink distributors in the U.S.

In order to help meet UAR's interests, he will indicate that Coca Cola is prepared to build a concentrate mixing plant in the UAR which would then be the source of supply for the rest of the Arab world. In this way the UAR's balance of payments would be helped and Cairo would be acquiring some additional capital.

Since Coca Cola also owns Sunkist, in addition they would be prepared to provide technical assistance to any UAR interests desiring to build plants to process UAR citrus fruits, either for domestic consumption or export. They are not prepared to put capital into such an enterprise, since Egypt's citrus growing is too dispersed for economic operations. But they figure that nevertheless the UAR might be interested in citrus processing as a possible export item or as a come-on for modernizing the citrus industry.

I briefed him on the complexity of our relations with Cairo, recalled our own food supply problems, and indicated we were exploring on the Hill what steps we could take on behalf of the UAR without jeopardizing other aspects of our economic development and assistance programs elsewhere.

DECLASSIFIED
E.O. 12356, Sec. 3.4
NLJ 91-421
By ___ NARA, Date 1-12-93

~~CONFIDENTIAL~~

COPY LBJ LIBRARY

78

a potential boycott of Coke by the Arab League, which was a response to the opening of a Coca-Cola bottling plant in Israel.

The corporate giant met with the US government to discuss the possibility of a meeting with Egyptian President Nasser in order to reach an agreement with the Arab League. Coke execs proposed to create separate production and labeling for Arab and Israeli Coke, a solution which was not implemented in 1956, but is the practice today.

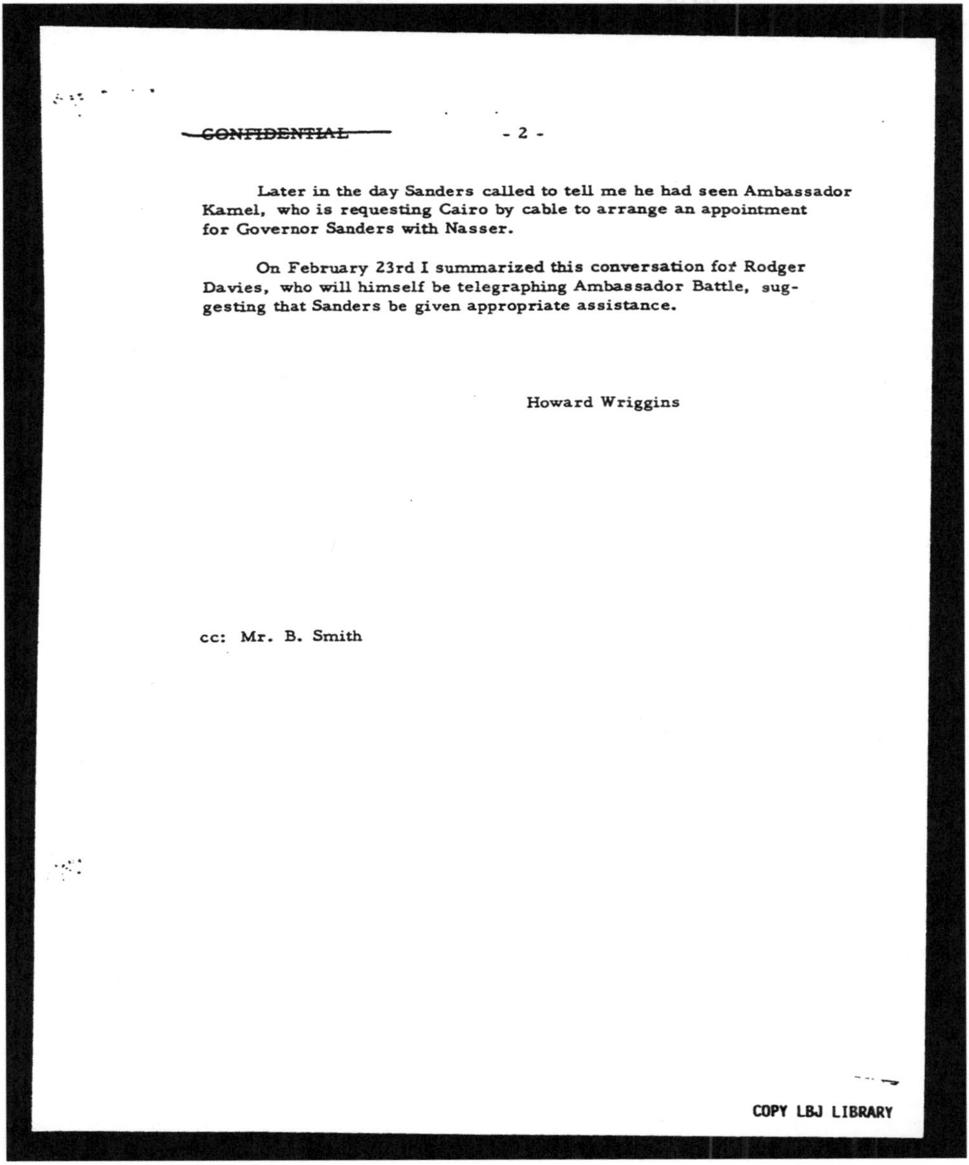

~~CONFIDENTIAL~~ - 2 -

Later in the day Sanders called to tell me he had seen Ambassador Kamel, who is requesting Cairo by cable to arrange an appointment for Governor Sanders with Nasser.

On February 23rd I summarized this conversation for Rodger Davies, who will himself be telegraphing Ambassador Battle, suggesting that Sanders be given appropriate assistance.

Howard Wriggins

cc: Mr. B. Smith

MEMORANDUM FOR MR. ROSTOW:
CAPITALISM AS FOREIGN POLICY

When Coca-Cola executives walked into the White House in February of 1967, they knew exactly what they wanted. Facing an impending boycott of their product in the Middle East, the global corporation needed the US government's help to circumvent a crisis of their brand.

The company had a direct line to the White House, and knew that at the very least the President and his cabinet would pave the way for Coke execs to meet with the highest ranking public officials in the US and the Middle East.

At first glance, this memo is a textbook example of how the United States government holds the hand of global corporations, helping them navigate foreign relations and secure profit.

Yet, the "Memo to Walt Rostow" is more complicated than that. Yes, Coca-Cola executives can call up the assistant for National Security Affairs and request the state's help in negotiating with governments overseas. But the document also shows that the US government was not particularly enthusiastic about helping the cola brand, in part because of the very specific political relations between the U.S. and Egypt.

When the background of the document comes into focus, Coca-Cola's meeting in the White House becomes not an instance of the US government supporting a single corporation because of personal ties or the possibility of profit. Rather, this meeting was part of a larger Cold War-era government goal to advance the spread of capitalism in the developing world.

In August of 1968, Arab League states implemented a boycott against Coca-Cola. As the memo recalls, the impetus for the boycott was the opening of a Coke bottling plant in Israel. Since 1948 the Arab League has boycotted all Israeli-made goods and companies, including U.S.-based corporations producing goods in Israel.

During 1966, Coca-Cola tried its best to avoid doing business in Israel, declining to sell its concentrate to an Israeli bottling plant. In their minds, sacrificing the huge Middle East market for one Israeli bottling plant was a bad business decision, not a political one.

But, as described in the document, Coca-Cola eventually relented, "only after great pressure mounted by friends of Israel through Jewish grocery stores and soft drink distributors in the US." These groups called the soda company anti-Semitic and argued that if the island of Cyprus was big enough for a bottling plant, so was Israel.

A boycott within the United States was unthinkable for Coca-Cola. To avoid this, Coke granted the franchise to an Israeli bottler, then appealed to the United States government for help in lobbying the Arab League with their latest idea—create separate and dissociated production facilities for Arab and Israeli Coke.

جامعة الدول العربية

THE LEAGUE OF ARAB STATES
Formed in Cairo, Egypt on 22 March 1945

The League of Arab States, also called the Arab League, is an umbrella organization comprising 23 Middle Eastern and African countries and entities. The purpose of the league has been to connect the Arab nations along political, cultural, economic, and social lines. Similar to the United Nations and the European Union, the League of Arab States has coordinated efforts defensively and economically, including the boycotting of companies and corporations doing business with Israel, like Coca-Cola.

MEET THE ROSTOWS

Walt Rostow may have been a devoted capitalist, but his parents were lifelong socialists. So much so they named their children after their own socialist heroes (pictured right): Eugene Victor Debs Rostow, Ralph Waldo Emerson Rostow, and our friend, Walt Whitman Rostow.

Popular imagery would have it that only the children of conservatives rebel, becoming left-leaning hippies. But lefties raise children too ...and sometimes they become anti-communist developmentalists.

Coca-Cola wanted to "build a concentrate mixing plant in the UAR to supply for the rest of the Arab world." They hoped the separate bottling plants would be enough to stop the boycott. The Arab League didn't buy it, however, and went ahead with the boycott, which lasted until 1991.

Interestingly enough, while the plan to separate the soda's manufacturing and sales didn't work in 1967, in present-day Palestine and Israel, Coke has two separate labels and separate bottling plants for the same Coca-Cola concentrate. But at the time, the Arab League was uncompromising and Coke needed connections to government officials and ambassadors, particularly Egypt's.

To send word of their plan to the Arab world, Coca-Cola wanted to get to its most prominent leader—Egypt's president, outspoken pan-Arab nationalist Gamal Abdel Nasser—and explain to him how separate Coke facilities might work. Doing this required no less than three Executive Branch departments, two national governments, and two ambassadors—one on each side of the Atlantic.

The man who received the memo, Walt W. Rostow, was President Lyndon B. Johnson's Special Assistant for National Security Affairs (now known as the National Security Advisor). Rostow was a virulent anti-communist and an architect of the U.S. government's fight to spread capitalism throughout the developing world.

Indeed, Rostow made advancing capitalism the end goal of all government-run aid programs. Rostow 's entire career was focused on the idea that modernization of the developing world, aided by the US, would contain communism and bring peace through a global network of capitalist democracies. His most influential work, written while at MIT, was titled The Stages of Economic Growth: A Non-Communist Manifesto.

Rostow believed that communism was a perversion of a "natural" development trajectory that led from capitalism to a modern democracy. When a nation needed food or monetary aid, Rostow encouraged the United States to intervene because he believed that food aid and assistance with technological development—the modernization of infrastructure such as roads, phone lines, and power grids so that global corporations can do business more efficiently—would contain communism.

Of course he was also convinced that military intervention could become necessary to reorient a state towards capitalism, as in the case of Vietnam. Rostow's theories were incredibly influential, and both Presidents Kennedy and Johnson used them to create their diplomatic strategies for US-Egyptian relations. Certainly, Egyptian President Nasser and his US Ambassador Mustapha Kamel were familiar with Rostow's theories, as Egypt consistently renegotiated food aid by leveraging their relationship with the Soviet Union:

> **I briefed him on the complexity of our relations with Cairo, recalled our own food supply problems, and indicated we were exploring on the Hill what steps we could take on behalf of the UAR without jeopardizing other aspects of our economic development and assistance programs elsewhere.**

To say that relations between the US and Egypt were complex is a vast understatement. Because Gamal Abdel Nasser positioned himself as the leader of the Arab world, Kennedy sought his alliance, and although Johnson did not trust Nasser as Kennedy did, he begrudgingly maintained the relationship with him, knowing without it US influence in the region would be weakened, and the Soviet Union would gain a foothold. The United States' tactic was to provide the struggling Egyptian economy with food aid in exchange for Nasser's good will—or good behavior.

President Nasser did not make it easy, however, as he constantly spoke vehemently against US policies, particularly against Johnson's support for Israel. Nasser also sought and received military arms and monetary aid from the Soviet Union. Johnson did eventually revoke Egypt's food aid in 1965, but when the Egyptian economy fell apart a short while later, he reinstated it.

These tactics—food aid under threat, with conditions attached—are part and parcel of Rostow's theories. If the US had permanently revoked food aid from Egypt for its dealings with the Soviet Union, it would have cemented Nasser's alliance with the Soviet Union. Because Nasser was a leader of the Arab world, losing him to the Soviet Union would have been an unmitigated disaster.

And of course, Nasser knew all of this and played both sides of the field—often to the detriment of the Egyptian people. The US says the food aid was being revoked from "Egypt," but really it was the Egyptian people who were denied food aid from 1966 to 1975. Starving citizens have a pesky habit of revolting, though, and in 1977 Egyptians staged food revolts after the IMF requested the country reduce food subsidies that were keeping wheat and bread affordable.

A decade without food aid in a struggling economy, and the IMF's solution was to reduce—and eventually eliminate—subsidies altogether; this was untenable. The play for power among nations seldom takes into consideration the real lives of citizens.

The Memo to Mr. Rostow contains multiple histories and government policies, and at the center of all of them is the attempt by the US government throughout the post-War period to advance the spread of capitalism. The US government, as a capitalist democracy, believes US corporations are the first line of offense in the fight to advance capitalism and stave off communism.

This belief is the reason government officials encouraged Coca-Cola to pursue their interests in the Arab world at a time when the US was cutting food aid and diplomatic relations with Egypt; corporations are symbols and bearers of U.S. capitalist culture. According to Rostow, capitalism is but a predecessor to democracy. This memo is included here because it helps to clarify the relationship between the US government and corporate interests in a way that gets to the heart of how capitalist democracies have become so hegemonic in the West.

At times, global capital appears as an overwhelming conspiracy. The IMF and World Bank seem like shady financiers of the G8's secret society dealings; as workers' movements around the globe suffer from repression and threats of outsourcing, and Wal-Mart gets bigger and bigger, it is hard not to see it all as conspiratorial.

The puppets used by activists in anti-globalization protests are not pure theatrics, but physical metaphors of the idea that conglomerations of capital are both the puppets and the puppeteers of capitalism. Activists are attracted to this line of thinking because it makes it easier to conceptualize a reorientation of power: get rid of the conspirators, and the situation will change.

But delve into this memo's history, and what emerges is a more nuanced picture of the relationship between government and global capital, between international development projects and corporate interests. This history shows the US government does not so much support one corporation at a time, but supports through a variety of actions and reactions the spread of capitalist free markets.

Coca-Cola, aware they were a symbol of American culture and hence a symbol of American capitalist democracy for cola drinkers the world over, was attempting to cash in on the government's compulsive Cold War need to advance capitalism and thwart the spread of communism.

The history of this document may feel cumbersome; the interplay of foreign relations, diplomatic conflict, and corporate profit is complicated and dredges up parts of other conflicts, other theories. But these names and ideas pop up time and again; before the War on Terror there was the Cold War, and it took up much ideological space in US government policy, foreign and domestic.

The fight against communism was used to justify assisting corporations just as often as it was deployed to disarm the radical Left. Corporations fought the Cold War as the advance capitalist offense against communism, a symbolic and profitable presence. Now, during the Iraq war, corporations are literally fighting the war, with mercenary soldiers and outsourced interrogators.

COKE vs. PEPSI
THE BATTLE FOR THE WHITE HOUSE

From political advisors down to the vending machines at 1600 Pennsylvania Ave., Coca-Cola and Pepsi have had their foot in the Oval Office since Eisenhower. Presented here is a brief history of the cola wars and the White House.

TEAM PEPSI

Nixon - Before becoming President, Tricky Dick worked for Pepsi's law firm and acted as their international ambassador, jet-setting around the world expounding on the wonders of the world's #2 cola. Pepsi's boss Don Kendall took a page out of Woodruff's book and started grooming his man for the presidency, and went with Dick straight to the White House.

Ford - Gerald took everything over for Tricky Dick after Watergate, Pepsi insiders included. Coca-Cola took advantage, running commercial spots during Nixon's resignation and Ford's acceptance speeches, to remind the nation what a Pepsi man had done to the country.

Reagan - Regan brought Pepsi back to the White House, vending machines and all. And Pepsi helped keep the Gipper in office, sending their best men to do his 1984 campaign ads. Riding each other's coattails to the top, Reagan and Pepsi were the choice of a New Generation.

Bush I - This former CIA chief and VP to the Gipper made sure everyone knew he was continuing the Legacy. To prove it, his inauguration parade was led by Pepsi trucks handing out free samples. Just think about that for a second.

Eisenhower - The only Republican on this list to choose The Real Thing, Ike showed his Coke love from the beginning of his presidency. After Ike used Army resources to parachute cokes to troops in World War II, Coca-Cola boss man Bob Woodruff supported Ike's bid for the White House, and remained his close confidant, advisor and golf buddy.

Kennedy - Camelot was the beginning of the two-party, two-cola system. Coke boss Woodruff kept himself in the White House by having Kennedy appoint Coca-Cola insiders as presidential advisors. The President even offered Woodruff an ambassadorship. He demurred, accepting an autographed JFK photo instead.

Johnson - LBJ carried on JFK's mission, and his rolodex. In fact, he was closer to Coca-Cola's boss than even Ike was. The night Martin Luther King, Jr was assassinated, LBJ and Woodruff were drinking together in the White House. Only it wasn't coke. Though it was a Coka-Cola jet that LBJ ordered to have Corretta Scott King taken to the funeral.

Carter - This Georgia politician was a Coke man all the way: best buds with Coke's prez, he flew in Coke jets, rode in Coke limos, and hired Coke ad men. He then installed Coke vending machines in the White House, Coke executives in his cabinet, and signed Coke tax breaks into law.

Clinton - Bill's political mentor owned a Coke bottling plant, so it's no surprise he brought Coke back to the White House. He chugged Cokes around the world, from McDonalds to overseas bottling plants, Bill used Coke photo-ops to prove he was an average American and a business-friendly Democrat.

Bush II - Ever the renegade and lover of big business, Dubya bucked all previous trends, rules and laws attached to the presidency. When it came to the Cola Wars, Bush didn't choose sides, he chose to take large sums of money from both cola companies, and fought for corporate tax loopholes domestically and abroad for both corporations.

COLANIZATION

...orld one bottle at a ...easy. From commies ...ders, and even those ...ng French, everyone ...es. Collected here are ...hts from Coca-Cola's ...of global domination.

Coca-Cola is far too large for the Earth alone. At a quarter-million dollars, Coca-Cola sent a dispenser into space with the Discovery space shuttle.

In 1970s Guatemala murder was called "Coca-Cola." Union leaders were terrorized and murdered under the direction of a Texan bottling plant owner. Of course Coke wasn't responsible, they simply licensed the operation. What could they do?

In Cuba, Batista loved it. As did Castro, who nationalized it. Later, Coke secretly met with him during the Carter administration to change his mind.

Not one to learn a lesson, Coca-Cola has again stood by (read: made money) as union leaders at Colombian bottling plants have been tortured and killed since the 1990s.

...oca-Colas consumed per capita in 2007

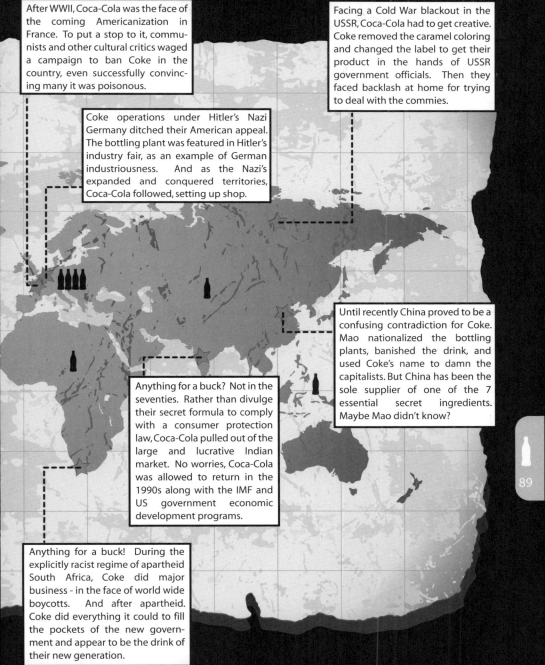

After WWII, Coca-Cola was the face of the coming Americanization in France. To put a stop to it, communists and other cultural critics waged a campaign to ban Coke in the country, even successfully convincing many it was poisonous.

Facing a Cold War blackout in the USSR, Coca-Cola had to get creative. Coke removed the caramel coloring and changed the label to get their product in the hands of USSR government officials. Then they faced backlash at home for trying to deal with the commies.

Coke operations under Hitler's Nazi Germany ditched their American appeal. The bottling plant was featured in Hitler's industry fair, as an example of German industriousness. And as the Nazi's expanded and conquered territories, Coca-Cola followed, setting up shop.

Until recently China proved to be a confusing contradiction for Coke. Mao nationalized the bottling plants, banished the drink, and used Coke's name to damn the capitalists. But China has been the sole supplier of one of the 7 essential secret ingredients. Maybe Mao didn't know?

Anything for a buck? Not in the seventies. Rather than divulge their secret formula to comply with a consumer protection law, Coca-Cola pulled out of the large and lucrative Indian market. No worries, Coca-Cola was allowed to return in the 1990s along with the IMF and US government economic development programs.

Anything for a buck! During the explicitly racist regime of apartheid South Africa, Coke did major business - in the face of world wide boycotts. And after apartheid. Coke did everything it could to fill the pockets of the new government and appear to be the drink of their new generation.

RECOMMENDED READING:

Spaces of Global Capitalism: Towards a Theory of Uneven Geographical Development
by David Harvey (New York, NY: Verso, 2006)

The Global Cold War: Third World Interventions and the Making of Our Times
by Odd Arne Westad (New York, NY: Cambridge University Press, 2007)

CONFIDENTIAL
COCA-COLA
FIREBOMB

7

ᴛʜᴇDOCUMENTS

Presented here are five declassified documents that show Coca-Cola on the losing end of some people power. FBI and CIA files and memos describe the attacks on Coca-Cola as part of routine national security briefs. These attacks on Coca-Cola are reported alongside information about attacks waged directly against the United States government.

Below is a brief guide to the five documents.

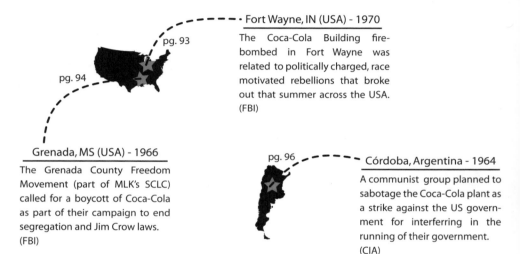

Fort Wayne, IN (USA) - 1970

The Coca-Cola Building fire-bombed in Fort Wayne was related to politically charged, race motivated rebellions that broke out that summer across the USA. (FBI)

Grenada, MS (USA) - 1966

The Grenada County Freedom Movement (part of MLK's SCLC) called for a boycott of Coca-Cola as part of their campaign to end segregation and Jim Crow laws. (FBI)

Córdoba, Argentina - 1964

A communist group planned to sabotage the Coca-Cola plant as a strike against the US government for interferring in the running of their government. (CIA)

Cali, Colombia - 1965

Communist revolutionary insurgents planted a bomb on the door-step of the Coca-Cola bottling plant. (CIA)

pg. 100

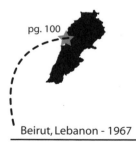

Beirut, Lebanon - 1967

The Coca-Cola building was set on fire by demonstrators targeting foreign supporters of Israel; Coca-Cola had recently agreed to open a bottling plant in Israel. (CIA)

MIDWEST

CHICAGO, ILLINOIS

On September 4, seventy-five members of The Disciples street gang marched peacefully to the Seventh District Police Department in protest of alleged police harassment. When the police refused to hear their protests, a rock and bottle throwing melee erupted. Twenty Disciples members were arrested for obstructing traffic and one police officer was injured by a thrown brick.

****

Two incidents of assaults on police occurred on September 5. One detective was shot at five times in Penn Central Station but was not wounded. One officer was fired on in his car on Chicago's South side. Both policemen returned fire, but the assailants escaped without injuries.

****

On September 7, a police officer shot and killed a member of the Disciples gang after he fired five shots at the officer's squad car.

FORT WAYNE, INDIANA

Early in the morning of September 5, fifty Negro youths gathered and threw a firebomb at the Coca Cola Building, causing some exterior damage. Police were called to disperse the crowd. Shortly afterwards, five additional fire-bombings occurred; one of them caused extensive damage to an A&P. Eight police cars were damaged and one officer was injured in the disturbance. The mayor of Fort Wayne imposed a curfew and the National Guard was placed on standby.

A transmission station was firebombed and completely destroyed early September 6. There were three reports of sniping at police. As of 3:00 a.m. on September 7, police had made forty-one arrests, and the city lifted the curfew later the same day.

DE WITT, IOWA

On September 5, a hand grenade simulator was thrown into the DeWitt police station. The explosion broke three windows, damaged two doors and injured two policemen. A suspect is in custody.

DeWitt is twenty miles north of Davenport, Iowa.

93

Fort Wayne, IN (USA) - 1970

5-141 (6-2-65)
OFFICE OF THE DIRECTOR

(27) 67

UNITED STATES DEPARTMENT OF JUSTICE

FEDERAL BUREAU OF INVESTIGATION

August 18, 1966

BY LIAISON

Honorable Marvin Watson
Special Assistant to the President
The White House
Washington, D. C.

K

Dear Mr. Watson:

       For your information, I am enclosing
a communication which may be of interest to you.

       Upon removal of the enclosure, if
classified, this transmittal form becomes
unclassified.

       Sincerely yours,

John Edgar Hoover
Director

Enc.
A copy of the enclosed has been furnished
to the Attorney General.

94

DEMONSTRATIONS CONTINUE IN GRENADA, MISSISSIPPI

   Demonstrations continued in Grenada, Mississippi, yesterday, under the sponsorship of the Southern Christian Leadership Conference in furtherance of the efforts of Negroes to demand equal access to public facilities and to encourage voter registration.

   Leon Hall of the Southern Christian Leadership Conference advised that Negroes distributed leaflets during the afternoon urging Negroes in Grenada not to buy products of the Coca-Cola Bottling Company because of that company's refusal to install an automatic dispensing machine in the Bell Flower Baptist Church. Following the meeting at St. Vincent's Chapel in Grenada,

-2-

Alphonso Harris of the Southern Christian Leadership Conference led a group of approximately 184 individuals, 60 per cent of whom were juveniles and four of whom were white, at about 9:00 p.m. from the chapel to the city square. The demonstrators circled the city square twice before returning to the chapel where a short rally was held. There were a small number of white spectators in the area of the demonstration. The marchers were again escorted by officers of the Mississippi Highway Safety Patrol and the Grenada Police Department. There were no incidents and no arrests were made.

95

Grenada, MS (USA) - 1966

CENTRAL INTELLIGENCE AGENCY

Intelligence Information Cable

COUNTRY	ARGENTINA	Content UNCLASSIFIED per 058375
		TDCS DB-315/01586-64
DATE OF INFO.	1 DECEMBER 1964	c 29 NOV 1976
		DISTR. 7 DECEMBER 1964

SUBJECT

PLAN BY COMMUNIST TERRORIST GROUP TO ABDUCT
AMERICAN CONSUL IN CORDOBA

PLACE & DATE ACQ.

REF   IN 36855

SOURCE
AND
APPRAISAL

FIELD REPORT NO.

TO ARMY STAFF COMM: EXCLUSIVE FOR ACSI, GENERAL DOLEMAN; NAVY DNI,
ADMIRAL TAYLOR; AIR FORCE AFCIN, GENERAL THOMAS
TO DIA : EXCLUSIVE FOR GENERAL CARROLL
TO STATE : NO DISTRIBUTION EXCEPT TO MR. THOMAS L. HUGHES

1. (HEADQUARTERS COMMENT: TDCSDB-315/01268-64, 3 NOVEMBER 1964,
REPORTED THAT A TERRORIST GROUP OF THE COMMUNIST PARTY OF ARGENTINA (PCA)
HAD PINPOINTED THE HOMES OF ALL UNITED STATES GOVERNMENT PERSONNEL IN
CORDOBA AND WAS PLANNING TO ABDUCT AN IMPORTANT OFFICIAL LIVING IN AN
ISOLATED AREA SOON. SEE, ALSO, TDCSDB-315/01305-64. THE INFORMATION
BELOW WAS ACQUIRED FROM THE SAME SOURCE.)

2. THE TARGET FOR ABDUCTION BY THE TERRORIST GROUP IS THE AMERICAN
CONSUL IN CORDOBA. THE PURPOSE IS TO AGITATE PUBLIC OPINION. THE ABDUCTION
WILL NOT TAKE PLACE SOON, AND THE ORDER NOT TO COMMIT VIOLENCE STILL STANDS.

SANITIZED COPY

DIR						GROUP 1
STATE/INR (HUGHES ONLY)	DIA	ARMY/ACSI	NAVY	AIR		
			DDI			EX O

3. ACCORDING TO THE PLAN, THE CONSUL IS TO BE ABDUCTED, THE PRESS WILL BE INFORMED, AND THE CONSUL WILL THEN BE RELEASED IN HIS UNDERPANTS. PROPAGANDA FLIERS ARE TO BE DISTRIBUTED EXPLAINING THAT THE ABDUCTION WAS CARRIED OUT TO "REPUDIATE YANKEE ACTIONS AGAINST CUBA AND OTHER FREE NATIONS."

4. INFORMATION ON THE LAYOUT OF THE CONSUL'S HOME IS TO BE SUPPLIED BY HIS GARDENER, OR FORMER GARDENER, WHO IS A MEMBER OF THE PCA.

5. THE SECOND TARGET OF THE GROUP WILL BE THE COCA-COLA PLANT, WHICH WILL BE SABOTAGED AS A SIGN OF PROTEST "AFTER THE UNITED STATES INTERVENES IN THE AFFAIRS OF SOME FREE NATION."

6. FIELD DISSEM: STATE (CORDOBA AND BUENOS AIRES), CINCSO (GENERAL O'MEARA ONLY).

END OF MESSAGE

97

Córdoba, Argentina – 1964

PRESS INFORMATION RELATING TO
INSURGENCY AND COUNTERINSURGENCY:
LATIN AMERICA

5 February 1965

OFFICE OF CENTRAL REFERENCE
Foreign Documents Division
CENTRAL INTELLIGENCE AGENCY
2430 E St., NW., Washington 25, D. 'C.

/<

C O L O M B I A

I. INSURGENCY AND COUNTERINSURGENCY

A. Terrorist Activities

1. Bombs Explode in Cali

DAS and F-2 agents are investigating two terrorist offenses
which occurred in Cali within 50 minutes of each other on
28 January. At 0020, a bomb exploded on the doorstep of the Coca-
Cola bottling plant, breaking windows and causing other damage.
The night watchman reported that he had seen three men drive by
in a red Willys jeep with a canvas top and throw the bomb at the
door. At 0110 another time bomb exploded in front of the
Colombia Club Grill, breaking windows in the building and in
neighboring houses. It was reported that one suspect, whose name
was not reported, had been arrested in connection with the
bombings. (Bogota, El Tiempo, 29 Jan 65)

2. Bomb Set in US Embassy

On 29 January, a bomb was discovered in one of the offices
of the US Embassy in Bogota. The bomb, which was found at 1800
hours, was made up of 15 sticks of dynamite, a clock and a special
mechanism, with magneto, and was set to go off at 1830. Two
cleaning women, Concha de Cortes and Tilsia Leal, found the bomb
which was in a box on the floor. Several crudely printed leaflets
were also found in the box, as well as an invoice carrying the
address of a manufacturing establishment.

[The following is a translation of one of the leaflets found
in the box containing the bomb.]

Thomas Mann is coming to Colombia:

To review the American troops stationed in Colombia.

To increase the massacres against the Colombian people,
especially against the Marquetalia, 26 September, Guayabero,
Pato, Jose Antonio Galan and Santa Barbara guerrilla fronts.

12

99

Cali, Colombia - 1965

1.3(a)(4)

1.3(a)(4)

CENTRAL INTELLIGENCE AGENCY
Directorate of Intelligence
10 June 1967

INTELLIGENCE MEMORANDUM

Arab-Israeli Situation Report
(As of 8:00 PM EDT)

1.   The Soviet Union has requested an emergency
meeting of the Security Council for 9:00 PM EDT.

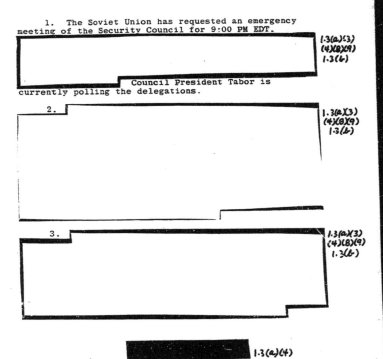

1.3(a)(3)
(4)(8)(9)
1.3(b)

Council President Tabor is
currently polling the delegations.

2.

1.3(a)(3)
(4)(8)(9)
1.3(b)

3.

1.3(a)(3)
(4)(8)(9)
1.3(b)

1.3(a)(4)

4. The US Mission to the UN has reported that corridor conversations with a number of Arab representatives reveal a noteworthy degree of similarity in Arab thinking regarding the US attitude toward Israel. There seems to be a strong feeling among the Arabs that the US has departed from a role of non-alignment and that we are favoring Israel. They cite evidence such as "managing" the US press to soft pedal the torpedoing of a US naval vessel, failure to exercise "well-known US influence" to stop the Israeli advance into Syria, Jordan and Egypt, and favoritism in US press reporting on the side of Israel.

5.

6. In Lebanon, a number of separate mobs roamed the streets of Beirut today, hurling rocks at the Soviet embassy, setting fire to a Coca Cola bottling plant, and storming the main gate of the American University. The army prevented the demonstrators from reaching their main objectives, the US and UK embassies, and a curfew was effectively imposed shortly after noon.

Beirut, Lebanon - 1967

BUY THE WORLD A COKE

RADICAL INTERNATIONAL
RESISTANCE AND COCA-COLA

The 1960s are well known for being a time of social upheaval, a single decade during which centuries-old race, class, gender, and sexual norms were put into question on a broad scale. All of that social change occurred through myriad small actions, miniature rebellions which for the most part have not entered the historical record.

The documents on the previous pages illustrate what happens when a global corporation, Coca-Cola, is on the receiving end of some of the people power for which the 1960s are famous.

The documents are bursting with the stories of resistance throughout the world during the 1960s, some of which can be teased apart by simply looking at the target of the action: Coca-Cola.

In the summer of 1966 police and officials looked on while nonviolent Mississippi Civil Rights demonstrators were terrorized and brutalized by white mobs led by the Ku Klux Klan. As a response, Coca-Cola and other companies complicit with segregation and Jim Crow laws were boycotted.

In the summer of 1970 race-related rebellions broke out across the United States as the demand for equality and freedom reached a fever pitch. As part of this rebellion, workers firebombed a Coke bottling plant.

Radicals organized resistance to the U.S. government's covert campaign of regime change in Latin America, which worked to arm rebels and assassinate leftist leaders. Coca-Cola bottling plants were bombed as symbols of American imperialism.

And in the Middle East the United States was embroiled in the fight over the state of Israel and was facing resistance to its imperialistic coveting of natural resources and strategic military locations. This time, the bottling plant was set ablaze by demonstrators.

To find Coca-Cola in the middle of all of this upheaval, violence, and resistance is not surprising. As you read in the last chapter, the United States government regularly gave support to Coca-Cola. And because Coca-Cola was both a direct benefactor of the United States government and one of the most recognizable symbols of American culture, it was also a target for resistance to U.S. policies and actions.

Domestically, this meant Civil Rights and Black Power movements targeted Coke for its explicit and tacit support of white supremacy. Abroad, Coca-Cola met resistance as an arm of U.S. imperialism.

The documents from Grenada, Mississippi and Fort Wayne, Indiana are evidence of a long struggle. Each document reveals FBI surveillance, and a government interest in "racial incidents" in the U.S. The FBI's interests did not lie in addressing white supremacy and racism, but in controlling and defeating political action and resistance.

Newspaper accounts from Grenada, Mississippi report that one week before the Grenada memo was authored, FBI agents stood by as "whites bombarded Negro demonstrators with rocks, bottles, and pipes." Local police purposefully kept their backs towards the KKK-led mob, watching and laughing as bricks and pipes struck Civil Rights demonstrators.

The FBI did not intervene to stop the brutal terrorism, but did continue to surveil members of Martin Luther King Jr's Southern Christian Leadership Conference (SCLC) who were in Mississippi to end Jim Crow segregation. Coca-Cola was the target of a boycott for their role in supporting segregation.

Four years later, a generation of activists who grew up witnessing the terrorism described above, as well as the assassinations of Martin Luther King, Jr., Malcolm X, and Fred Hampton, had no patience for white supremacy or terrorism. The rebellion in Fort Wayne, Indiana was one of hundreds of rebellions that broke out across the United States.

During these uprisings, the FBI investigated and arrested demonstrators for any acts of violence. However, that didn't stop Fort Wayne workers from firebombing the Coca-Cola bottling plant in response to racist hiring and workplace policies. Coca-Cola was not only a symbolic target, but was targeted by labor activists for offering low-paying exploitative jobs.

In Cordoba, Argentina, Communist rebels sabotaged the Coca-Cola bottling plant. And in Cali, Columbia, a bomb was exploded on the doorstep of their bottling facility. Latin America was a locus of anti-imperialism, as the U.S. government fought its war on Communism in Latin America through covert CIA operations to interfere with and overthrow leftist governments.

The CIA aggressively operated in Guatemala, Cuba, Brazil, Bolivia, Chile, Nicaragua, Argentina, and Colombia. Communist groups and rebels fought back against US government officials and symbols of US imperialism, such as Coca-Cola.

The U.S. government and the CIA were also busy in the Middle East. In response to the construction of the Israeli Coca-Cola plant described in the previous chapter, demonstrators set fire to the Coke bottling plant in Beirut, Lebanon. This action was part of a larger rebellion against foreign support of Israel and US imperialism.

While these actions took place over time and throughout the world, it is clear that the Coca-Cola corporation operates as a sort of symbolic intermediary. Unable to directly affect the United States government, resistance groups chose a symbol of American cultural and economic imperialism, and by so doing did get the attention of the United States. government, as these declassified documents prove.

RECOMMENDED READING:

The Darker Nations: A People's History of the Third World
by Vijay Prashad (New York, NY: New Press, 2008)

How Capitalism Underdeveloped Black America
by Manning Marable (Cambridge, MA: South End Press, 1999)

SECRET REAGAN 8
BROWNIES &
HYRDOPONICS

ᴛʜᴇDOCUMENTS

Both of the documents presented here are official White House transcripts of President Ronald Reagan's meetings with two heads of state. Each head of state poses a problem to President Reagan, hoping that perhaps the US might contribute its vast resources to help solve Mexico's widespread poverty, or the specter that population growth might outstrip food supplies. In both transcripts, President Reagan offers the same solution: the free market. To both heads of state Reagan provides an illustrative example of free market solutions... starring food.

~~SECRET~~

0178

THE WHITE HOUSE

WASHINGTON

~~SECRET~~

MEMORANDUM OF CONVERSATION

SUBJECT: Private Meeting Between President Reagan and
                  President de la Madrid of Mexico (U)

PARTICIPANTS: The President
                  President de la Madrid of Mexico

DATE, TIME   January 3, 1986
AND PLACE: 11:00 a.m., Governor's Palace, Mexicali, B.C.

                  (President de la Madrid spoke in Spanish,
                  with Mrs. Italia Morayta serving as
                  interpreter)

After an exchange of pleasantries <u>President de la Madrid</u> asked what subjects President Reagan was interested in, adding that his own list was enormous. (C)

SECRET
- 4 -

The President said that, as far as economic issues were concerned, the United States had set an example with its recovery that couldn't be matched by even its European friends. Some European leaders had told him that they were so bound up with statism and regulations that they couldn't follow the U.S. example and give freer rein to private enterprise. He said that

SECRET

SECRET
- 5 -.

the Federal Government had given greater leeway to the individual states in order to enable them to stimulate private investment in their own ways. (C)

The President recalled the example of a young lady who had graduated from college with a degree in classical piano, only to develop tendonitis in her hands to such a degree that she couldn't play anymore. Some of her relatives, remembering the delicious brownies she had baked in the past, and in an effort to lift her spirits, suggested that she bake some and sell them in neighborhood grocery stores. Rachel Brown Brownies were now sold in gourmet stores and restaurants, as well as in airlines, and the young lady grossed $2.5 million last year, employing hundreds of people. A case such as this, where no major capital investment was required, was a good example of what could be done. (U)

SECRET

THE WHITE HOUSE

WASHINGTON

MEMORANDUM OF CONVERSATION

SUBJECT: Meeting with Prime Minister De Mita of Italy

PARTICIPANTS: U.S.
                  The President
                  Secretary of State, George P. Shultz
                  Secretary of the Treasury, James Baker III
                  Secretary of Defense, Frank C. Carlucci
                  Kenneth M. Duberstein, Deputy Chief of Staff
                  Colin L. Powell, Assistant to the President
                       for National Security Affairs
                  Marlin Fitzwater, Assistant to the President
                       for Press Relations
                  W. Allen Wallis, Under Secretary of State for
                       Economic Affairs
                  Rozanne L. Ridgway, Assistant Secretary of State
                       for European and Canadian Affairs
                  Maxwell M. Rabb, U.S. Ambassador to Italy
                  Charles Z. Wick, Director, USIA
                  Barry F. Lowenkron, Director, European and
                       Soviet Affairs, NSC (Notetaker)
                  Neil Seidenman, Interpreter, Department of State

                  ITALY
                  Prime Minister Ciriaco De Mita
                  Foreign Minister Giulio Andreotti
                  Rinaldo Petrignani, Ambassador to the U.S.
                  Bruno Bottai, Secretary General of the Ministry
                       of Foreign Affairs
                  Luigu Goudobono Cavalchini, Chief of Staff, MFA
                  Umberto Vattani, Diplomatic Advisor (Notetaker)
                  Mario Arcelli, Economic Advisor
                  Giuseppe Sangiorgi, Prime Minister's Assistant
                  Vivina Bonaccorsi (Interpreter)

DATE, TIME   June 14, 1988, 11:30 a.m. - 1:30 p.m.
AND PLACE: Oval Office, Cabinet Room and Residence

At the initial tete-a-tete the President welcomed Prime
Minister De Mita, recalling his meetings with him in 1984 and
in 1986 when the Prime Minister came as the head of the
Christian Democratic Party.

SECRET
Declassify on: OADR

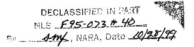

Foreign Minister Andreotti then raised the issue of world
population by saying that by the year 2001, it will have
doubled while land available for growing crops would continue
to decrease. He cautioned that countries with low agriculture
costs such as the U.S. should not decrease their production too
much.

11

President Reagan responded by referring to Malthus, saying that
had his prediction been correct, there would not have been
enough food to feed the world today. Secretary Shultz
described Malthus's "Iron Law," that there would be only so
much food available and that this amount would regulate the
size of the population. The President mentioned that in a
campaign stop at Illinois, he had toured a great glass building
with rows and rows of lettuce growing without soil, and every
morning, truck after truck would carry the lettuce out to
market.

Foreign Minister Andreotti asked, "but how much does this
production cost?" The President responded "I do not know if it
costs any more than garden lettuce." Secretary Shultz said the
point was that hydroponic lettuce competed successfully in the
market place without a subsidy. Foreign Minister Andreotti
then recalled his tour of an agricultural display at the Epcot
Center, and he reminded the President that in response to
Malthus, chemical fertilizers had been created.

BEHOLD!
THE FREE MARKET
RONALD REAGAN AND
FREE MARKET EVANGELISM

Ronald Reagan: so much has been written about him that it almost seems moot to write this now. Everyone has an opinion on Ronald Reagan. For some, he was the conservative grim reaper of the welfare state, whose rise marked the dawning of the neoliberal era. To conservatives, he is the apotheosis of fiscal responsibility, a model for all U.S. presidents in the new global economy.

To achieve this level of notoriety, Reagan dramatically slashed social programs such as welfare, subsidized childcare, and public housing. He cut taxes for the wealthiest Americans, and he paved the way, through deregulation, for the corporate outsourcing of jobs. But make no mistake: Reagan was a classist demagogue, a believer in the power of capitalism and the profit motive who preyed on the fears of the middle class—their fears that they were one missed mortgage payment away from poverty, or that they had more in common with people who used subsidized child care than those who paid nannies—to create a political climate in which people of modest means were completely Othered and reviled.

To justify these spending cuts, Reagan told stories that gave his policies a human element and constructed a set of core conservative values in which people who relied on government social programs were leeches on the system, taking away the middle class's hard-earned dollars. In these stories, the middle and working classes distinguish themselves by their "work ethic" and other meaningless capitalist values.

In this way, Reagan was like every other politician, spinning stories about what he learned from Jill the Baker, who has it hard because her insurance policy did not pay out, or Steve the Carpenter, who turned a workplace injury into an opportunity to go back to school. Politicians use these stories all the time.

The documents presented in this chapter involve these anecdotes, stories Reagan spun to bring humanity into policies, to show not only that they could be successful economically, but that they were good for people as well.

Reagan's stories are meant to show the beauty of the free market, and are meant both as lessons in human ingenuity and as cautionary tales. His words carry undercurrents of classism and are meant to impart fear.

In the documents presented here, "Reagan's Secret Brownies," and "Reagan's Secret Hydroponics," Reagan spins tales of free market success stories for world leaders. In these tales, downtrodden Americans use their ingenuity to pull themselves up by their bootstraps, using the capitalist market to solve their problems rather than relying on government social programs, such as Social Security Disability Insurance or agricultural subsidies.

The idea that it is nobler, more dignified, to pull yourself up by your bootstraps is a prolific one, and throughout his presidency Reagan's anecdotes in meetings and speeches centered on these kinds of tales. The bootstraps myth uses a capitalist logic that implies both that it is possible (and desirable) to rise in the class ranks, and that those who are able to do so deserve their success.

Reagan's story about Rachel's Brownies, told to the President of Mexico, is a case in point. The story he tells is true, although he misstates the name of the brownie company. There was indeed a woman prevented from following her dream of playing the piano who then built a small brownie fortune by securing a contract with United Airlines to be their exclusive brownie provider.

As Reagan tells it, the woman responsible for Rachel's Brownies is an example of capitalism at work; unhindered by excessive taxation and regulation, Rachel built her brownie empire with nothing but her injured joints. In telling this story to President de la Madrid, President Reagan was trying to convince the Mexican President to reform Mexico's Constitution to allow foreign investors to own land, namely, American hoteliers who were anxious to develop Baja, California, which is part of Mexico.

Reagan argues that although the majority of profit will leave the country, there will be plenty of room for small enterprises such as Rachel's Brownies—which require "no major capital investment"—because tourists are suckers for souvenirs. American corporations get the big money—profits from hotels and perhaps more importantly, land ownership—while Mexican entrepreneurs are relegated to running shops

DREAMS FOR BAJA

President Reagan then said that he had an additional subject to bring up, one that had been a dream of many years. He would stick his nose in and give some advice:

Baja California could be converted into one of the great resort centers of the world. He was sure that there were hotel chains which would be willing to invest the necessary capital, if they were sure that there was no danger of expropriation. If they could obtain ownership of the land, he was sure that they would build the hotels and beach cottages in an area that had both a great climate and great natural beauty. They would also provide a natural market for articles that tourists buy. He recalled that when he was Governor of California he attended many Governors' meetings, and remembered how he had liked the handicrafts he has received as gifts. He knew he was being presumptuous, but he suggested that Mexico study the possibility of changing its laws and customs on land ownership and consider a system such as that which had worked so well in the U.S.

The New York Times, Sunday, April 27, 1986
Mexico Pushes Tourism Anew

The Washington Post, Saturday, Spetember 12, 1987
Mexico Unveils Baja Resort Investment Plan

full of reproductions of stereotypical Mexican crafts and food.

Reagan deploys this tale to assert the right of American investors to build in Mexico; he believes capitalism prevails, and neither a constitution nor Mexico's deep-seated political norms about land ownership should stop its inevitable growth. Less than two years later, Mexico opened up Baja to investment.

In "Reagan's Secret Hydroponics," President Reagan is again trying to convince foreign leaders to deregulate and open up their markets. But what is truly remarkable about the document, a 1988 conversation between President Reagan and Italian Prime Minister Ciriaco de Mita, is how dismissive President Reagan is about the food crisis affecting the developing world.

Reagan suggests, again through an anecdote, that world leaders should look to the free market to solve the food crisis. His tale of the hydroponic lettuce growers is meant to point out to the Italian prime minister that "hydroponic lettuce competed successfully in the market without a subsidy."

"Without a subsidy" is the crux of free market capitalism. To produce lettuce without a subsidy means the farmers received no assistance from the government. A subsidy is government aid meant to take up the slack between what it actually costs to grow crops and what price wholesalers are willing to pay.

The U.S. government pays out these subsidies because prices are driven down, in part, by a globalized economy in which goods from overseas are often cheaper than those grown at home. Without subsidies, small farmers could not afford to grow food in the United States, which is seen as important to domestic security in addition to being beneficial to the Global South.

The developing world receives food aid in the form of grain from the United States, which benefits the U.S. because too much grain for sale will flood the market and drive costs down further, making agriculture completely unsustainable.

To avoid this economic collapse, the government buys the grain and sends it overseas. It is not only the United States which provides subsidies to its farmers—the European Union does so as well, ensuring that some farmers are able to profit off of their grain while others are paid to let their fields lay fallow.

Reagan's story of hydroponic lettuce, in this climate, engenders fear because it suggests that subsidies are a major obstacle to a truly free market. The balance of subsidies, grain aid, and other forms of government assistance, coordinated on a global scale, has always been precarious.

An Italian cabinet member asks Reagan not to "decrease their production too much," a plea for the United States not to reduce subsidies so much that the world grain market collapses. Reagan's tale of hydroponic lettuce immediately registers with the Italian cabinet members as problematic; they understood globalized agriculture as a messy, complicated business that could not be reduced to platitudes about lettuce grown in a warehouse.

But Reagan meant to impress upon them the power of free market ingenuity; hand in hand with that individualistic power, though, is a disempowerment of farmers in the face of a globalizing economy, and of people of modest means in the U.S. who use government social programs.

While Reagan was by no means the first free market evangelist, he did make significant headway for the cause in the United States with his cuts to domestic services and his enthusiastic embrace of foreign investment.

And Reagan's tales of free market food are the organizing narratives for free market capitalism, stories that breathe life into his policies by striking fear of the Other into the middle class and fear of economic world collapse into the hearts of foreign leaders.

Top: Ronald Reagan shaking hands with Mexican President de la Madrid
Bottom: Ronald Reagan shaking hands with Italian Prime Minister de Mita

TALKING HEADS
DEFENDERS OF CAPITALISM FINGER PUPPETS

Now you too can be a capitalist talking head! Use these finger puppets on one hand to distract family, friends, or enemies from seeing what you're doing with the other hand. Does someone need your help? Just put on the Ronald Reagan puppet and tell them to pull themselves up by their bootstraps. Want to aggressively assert your right to profit off the death and misfortune of others? Cheney and Rumsfeld have you covered. Or do you need to go really old-school, like a good 18th century industrialist? Put on the Adam Smith puppet and take what you need. We've even thrown in Walt Whitman Rostow (remember him from Chapter 6?), in case you encounter any Leftists who need to be reminded of what's really important: the bottom line.

DICK CHENEY

ADAM SMITH

WALT WHITMAN ROSTOW

119

RECOMMENDED READING:

Tear Down This Myth: How the Reagan Legacy Has Distorted Our Politics and Haunts Our Future
by Will Bunch (New York, NY: Free Press, 2009)

Bad Samaritans: The Myth of Free Trade and the Secret History of Capitalism
by Ha-Joon Chang (New York, NY: Bloomsbury Press, 2008)

A Brief History of Neoliberalism
by David Harvey (New York, NY: Oxford University Press, 2005)

Profit Over People: Neoliberalism & Global Order
by Noam Chomsky (New York, NY: Seven Stories Press, 1999)

EPILOGUE:

EXPOSING SECRETS

Government secrecy does not expose itself. Although the government does declassify documents, the process is archaic, slow, and opaque.

The public exposure of illegal government programs, so-called black prisons, and sanctioned torture more often comes from the efforts of courageous folks who have taken on the government in the pursuit of justice. Whistleblowers, radical lawyers, and activists have all worked to expose the worst kinds of government secrecy.

Occasionally, government secrecy is exposed from inside the bureaucratic maw. In 1971 famed whistleblower Daniel Ellsberg, a Pentagon insider, brought the United State occupation of Vietnam to its knees when he leaked the Pentagon Papers.

The Papers were a top-secret Pentagon report that detailed the strategic and deliberate misleading of the American public by the U.S. government, reaching all the way back to the presidency of Dwight D. Eisenhower in the 1950s.

Ellsberg, once called "the most dangerous man in America," faced down potential prison time, and even assassination, to expose vast government misdeeds in Southeast Asia and bring the Pentagon Papers to light.

The court system also brings government secrecy into the light of day. Often, radical lawyers have to fight for access to classified files in order to defend their clients. William Kunstler (1919-1995), for example, was a famed radical lawyer who defended Civil Rights activists, Black Panthers, and many other people targeted by secret, illegal government programs.

Kunstler was also director of the American Civil Liberties Union (ACLU) and cofounder of the Center for Constitutional Rights (CCR).

These organizations continue to expose government secrecy when it impedes free people, movements, and justice. Recently, the ACLU and CCR have exposed the United States government's use of torture in the War on Terror.

Yet, the court system may not be enough to expose government secrets. In these cases, direct action has accomplished what legal means failed to do. In 1971, an anonymous group of people calling themselves the Citizens' Commission to Investigate the FBI broke into an FBI office in Media, Pennsylvania and stole over 1,000 classified documents.

The group distributed the documents to the press, exposing the FBI's illegal COINTELPRO. For the first time, the American public learned of the FBI's wiretapping, manipulation of media, and infiltration of civil rights and Black Power activist groups. These citizens, who mailed the stolen documents to US newspapers, exposed a war against the American people by the American government. COINTELPRO targeted activists, celebrities who supported the Black Panthers, teachers, students—anyone perceived as threat to the US government. And none of these people knew they were targets until these documents were revealed. Eventually, the exposure of this program led to hearings and to a closer monitoring of the FBI.

Today, the ease of document transmission via the internet, and websites such as Wikileaks.org increase the exposure of government secrecy by both insiders and outsiders. Wikileaks is an international crowd-sourced site for the public exposure of secrecy and has been a tremendous tool for those fighting for transparency in government and society.

Secret and illegal U.S. government programs and actions in the wars in Iraq and Afghanistan have been and continue to be exposed on the site, including top-secret video footage of civilians being killed with bombs.

Anyone can request declassified documents from the United States government using a Freedom of Information Act request. While the process takes some patience, many journalists and concerned citizens have successfully used FOIA requests to obtain information otherwise unavailable.

You can use the FOIA request template on the following page as a model for your request. Happy searching!

Agency Head (or Freedom of Information Act Officer)
Name of Agency
Address of Agency
City, State, Zip Code

Re: Freedom of Information Act Request

Dear _____:

This is a request under the Freedom of Information Act.

I request that a copy of the following documents (or documents containing the following information) be provided to me: (identify the documents or information as specifically as possible.)

In order to help to determine my status to assess fees, you should know that I am (insert a suitable description of the requester and the purpose of the request).

(Sample requester descriptions:
* a representative of the news media affiliated with the _____ newspaper (magazine, television station, etc.), and this request is made as part of news gathering and not for a commercial use.
* affiliated with an educational or noncommercial scientific institution, and this request is made for a scholarly or scientific purpose and not for a commercial use.
* an individual seeking information for personal use and not for a commercial use.
* affiliated with a private corporation and am seeking information for use in the company's business.)

(Optional) I am willing to pay fees for this request up to a maximum of $_____. If you estimate that the fees will exceed this limit, please inform me first.

(Optional) I request a waiver of all fees for this request. Disclosure of the requested information to me is in the public interest because it is likely to contribute significantly to public understanding of the operations or activities of the government and is not primarily in my commercial interest. (Include a specific explanation.)

Thank you for your consideration of this request.

Sincerely,

Name
Address
City, State, Zip Code
Telephone number (Optional)

INDEX

BE OUR "BEST FRIEND FOREVER"

Do you love what Microcosm publishes?
Do you want us to publish more great stuff?
Would you like to receive each new title as it's published?
If your answer is "yes!", then you should
subscribe to our BFF program. BFF
subscriptions help us pay for printing
new books and zines and ensure that we
can print more great material each
month! Every time we publish something
new we'll send it to your door!

Subscriptions are based on a sliding scale of
$10-30 per month! You'll get zines, books,
DVD, shirts, stickers, patches, and more!

microcosmpublishing.com/bff

* Minimum subscription period is 6 months.
Subscription begins the month after it is purchased. To receive more
than 6 months, add multiple orders to your quantity. The estimated
shipping weight is 110 ounces for every six month subscription.

Microcosm Publishing
222 S Rogers St. Bloomington, IN 47404
www.microcosmpublishing.com